SUPERTRAMP

THE STORY OF BRUCE

KEN RING

Copyright © Ken Ring 1999-2014
All rights reserved.
ISBN: 978-0-86467-004-5

Second Edition. Reprint of original work published in 1999 by Milton Press Ltd.

All rights reserved. No part of this book may be reproduced or transmitted in any form or by any means, electronic or mechanical, including photocopying, recording, or any information storage and retrieval system without prior written permission of the author.

DEDICATION

To my fellow travellers, Jude, Keri and Miri.

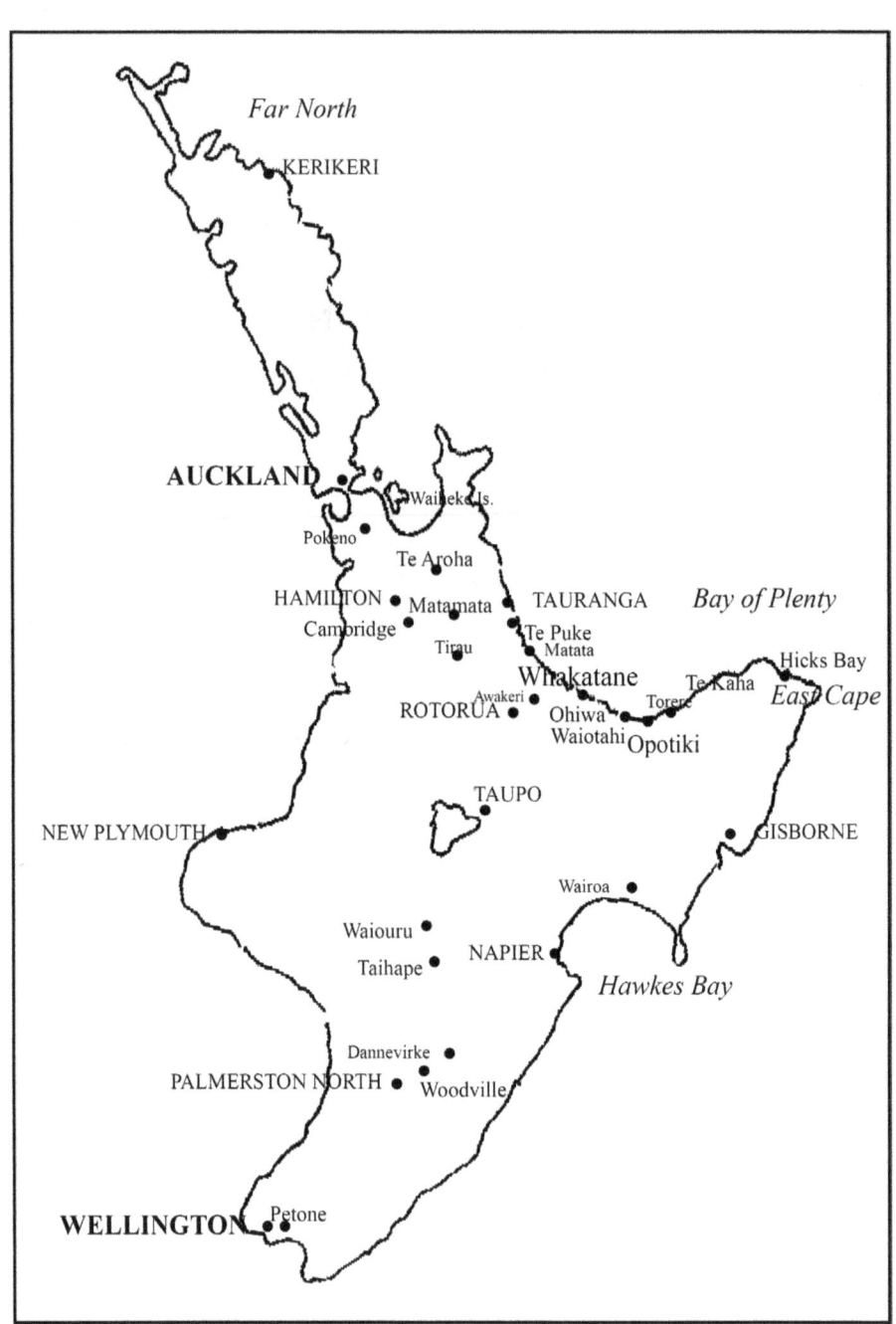

NORTH ISLAND OF NEW ZEALAND

Table Of Contents

An Encounter 1
Early Years 15
Farewell To The City 25
Camping Days 41
The Bottles 53
Working 65
Waiheke Island 81
Animals 93
Verbal Encounters 111
The Law 141
The Ohiwa Camp. 175
Fishing 189
Finding Food 211
Accidents and Illness 233
The Way of Life 241
End of The Road 265
Acknowledgements 281

Ken Ring

An Encounter

"I like camping under telegraph poles, so I can hear the singin' in the wires. It's one of Nature's sounds. Like the wind blown' a broken window pane."

It was a particularly hot February afternoon. I looked up from my workbench to see a dusty figure wheeling a gear-laden bike into the grassed area. He was bare-chested, with grey shorts, plastic sandals, and a beret; a very tanned body with a very white beard. It was a dramatic sight and I needed a break from the chemical smells of the leather dyes and polishes, so I went out the bus and wandered towards him, hailing from a polite distance.

'You must be hot!' He looked a bit bewildered. 'Would you like a drink?'

'Oh, don't mind if I do matey.'

But there was some hesitation as he entered the bus and sat down.

'You know this is the first bit of hospitality I've been offered in about two years.' It seemed a strange thing to say.

Well, his name was Bruce and he had come from Omana that day and was on his way north. There were wild vegetables he had to check on at Ohiwa and at Waikeri. At Hicks Bay he had just checked his taro plantation.. Once he started to talk he didn't stop. The stories kept coming. And kept coming.

He ate some cake and drank our tea, even though he complained about how he was unused to such food, and how he would quite likely be back-sliding now for about two weeks in terms of health.

As the light began to fade he offered to cook us a meal. We smiled. Oh sure. What with?

Bruce ran outside and took some gear off his bike. In seconds he'd started a fire out of twigs and driftwood on the beach in front of the bus. As the flames got going, he hauled over two nearby logs and carefully placed them so they effectively divided the blaze into three compartments. Apparently, on the most windward side was going to be the fast fryer, the middle was going to be the element on which to cook the pudding , and the leeside embers were the bread oven.

We didn't know what to make of him. Here was this tramp who was totally unknown to us a couple of hours earlier, who had in this moment become part of our world and was organizing a multi-course meal *out of nothing*.

Any doubts were rapidly dispelled. A stir-fry was under way from opossum meat and a pukeko he had found on the road, and wild vegetables. Opossum meat was okay, he explained, not too much damaged. And he always knew which ones were fresh, because he only picked up the ones not on the road for more than a day (thank goodness for that).

Afterwards there was a hot fruit dessert and still later yummy bread. How did he cook the bread? So obvious, when you saw. He just rolled up a ball of bread dough and threw it in the dying embers. By the time we had finished the other courses it was ready. Cut away the burnt black crust and eat the inside - yum! Tea too, from a billy, with tea bags that had been dried and reused a few times. Nothing wrong with it, if you don't mind your tea tasting rather strongly of tannin.

Later, more talking. I stayed up listening to him all night. He never faltered, never seemed to tire, never repeated anything and we kept going the next day, and by the next night I needed some sleep. Yet he seemed as fresh as ever. He stayed camped next to us another day, and then continued northwards.

What they call the East Coast in New Zealand is the monumentally rugged piece of coastline between .and East Cape. Halfway down is the sleepy town of Opotiki. I knew it as the centre of a farming district that woke up only on a Friday night when the farm lads cruised in for a change of scene. On weekdays folk walk up and down Main Street stopping so often to talk that no-one really seems to get to where they're going.

Four miles north of Opotiki is an empty patch called the

Waiotahi Domain. Beside this the Waiotahi River ends a journey that starts up in the misty Urewera foothills, ancestral home of the Tuhoe people. The river winds down from steep mountainous bush through the lush Waiotahi Valley with its deep greens, and finally to the sea. Beside the river mouth, on flat unkempt treeless ground, unlimited camping has traditionally been allowed. Consequently it was a favourite overnight stopping place for many, us included.

There was free fresh water, a toilet block and a lovely sandy beach that yielded endless shellfish for those in the know.

The river-mouth was not just the home of shellfish. Fish of all kinds too would gather, to taste the cooler fresh water that came rushing down from the hills to join the salt of the sea, to feed on the shellfish, and to travel upstream yearly to spawn where it was safer and warmer than in the wild ocean. And the fish attracted the fishermen, with their rods and tackle-boxes.

We were living on our bus: me and Jude and two children. The Domain suited us well. The net was always out and we found we could live mainly on seafood. In fact we caught too much, about six fish per day, mostly flounder and porori, so we were always giving it away. Opotiki was handy and good for supplies, and we were only about a mile from Reeves farm, on the shores of the tranquil Ohiwa Inlet, where we'd leased some land by his cowshed for growing vegetables. It was a great spot with black soil – the whole garden washed over regularly by high tides.

The bus was a travelling craft shop, I was turning out leather goods and bone and silver jewellery and Jude made and sold her beautiful macramé-and-shell belts and ornaments and her crocheted garments.

We would put out craft-shop signs and folk came on board. Not a day went by without some visitor or other, either from the campers passing through or the locals. We were always ready for strangers, and some were no doubt attracted by the smell of Jude's muffins and soup on the little wood-stove.

Many travellers came through that little spot; a family of real Romany gypsies in a truck, a few horse-drawn caravans trying to look like gypsies, a couple of tractor-pulled gypsy wagons, some arty house trucks, and many buses and caravans. In fact every way of being on the road and on the move was represented, plus the usual type of tramper with the overnight tent. At any one time there would be four or five lots of 'roadies' as well as ourselves, on the good old Waiotahi Domain.

Some were characters you wouldn't forget. I remember a harmonica-playing Texan who hitchhiked up and down the Coast getting work breaking-in horses. He told us about the traditional American Indian way of breaking them in, in which you don't tie the horse up or anything - you just sniff out over and over, which is hello in horse language. Apparently the wild horse then trusts you and lets you mount him. He was a lot in demand with the Maori East Coast farmers, because his method was more akin to the Maori way of doing things. Also he had a crazy Texan accent, which probably intrigued the horses too..

Then there was a sad man sleeping in his old car, determined to travel, having promised his late wife before she died that he would do the camping trip they had both dreamed about so much before she fell sick.

And the drovers, with hundreds of cattle and a couple of lean dogs, stopping to camp for a day or two to let the herd fatten on the green grass.

'Hey, don't give the dogs those bones.'

'Why not?'

'Aw, dogs won't work if you feed 'em.'

'So how do they eat?'

'They forage mate. This evening, watch them go, they'll be right'

He was right, of course. At sundown the dogs took off sniffing everywhere. They soon found the bones I must have accidentally left.

Then there was the old kuia (elderly lady) who strode in her high black gumboots, down from the hill across the dirt road on many a morning, carrying nothing but an empty flax basket. She'd tear strings of flax from the water's edge and join them into a longish line, take a fish-hook from her blouse and tie it on the end of the knotted line, bait the hook with pipis and cast it into the incoming tide. When she got two fish she put them in the flax basket, took off the hook which went back on her blouse, and threw the line away. Then she walked back up the hill carrying just the basket with the fish. Never said a word to anyone. And she always caught two fish. She could be standing between two anglers with expensive equipment who hadn't gotten anything all morning, but put her line in, get her fish and leave again, leaving the anglers speechless, fishless and annoyed.

We met some travellers two or three times, because they'd go up the coast and back again. We also befriended a few of the townspeople, like the area dairy inspector Gordon Rogers and his wife Kath, to whom we gave fish and in return were given heaps of vegetables and lovely home cooked meals whenever we went into town.

They were happy days, and times of plenty; lots to eat, good weather and good conversations around late night campfires.

The bus was a '47 OB Bedford, with a petrol motor. We were well set up; hot water system from a wetback around the woodburning stove, gas oven as well, loo, bath, bunks, 240 volt plus 12 volt electricity, all running from spare batteries and a generator. A smokehouse was on the roof, around the chimney outlet, with a built-on ladder to get up there. We carried bulk food, bulk supplies and didn't need to go near any township for at least a month. We even collected rainwater in two 50 gallon tanks.

The 70s were the beat generation. Around the area communes were becoming established. Young folk were dropping out of the city and going back to the land, with their ideals of simple living and their tapes of Eric Clapton. These commune folk had recently discovered the Coast - here was cheap land because many of the owners had vacated and gone to the cities where the work and big money was. The area was a bit neglected and in need of old-fashioned toil.

Certain weeds could be grown out of sight from the prying eyes of the authorities, and many travellers coming from the coast had a distinctly faraway look in their eyes. You never knew who was going to turn up next, and you learnt to expect anything.

There were people you met who passed you by and you thought nothing more of. Then there were some who stayed awhile, and danced with you for as long as that music played. And then there were a third category, who got under your skin and became embedded in your thoughts, in your bloodstream and become part of your very pith.

Why that should be is surely part of the mystery and adventure of this life. Like floating debris in a river, pieces come together and then together lock on. How it happens and why, is less important than the fact that it does. Sometimes a person's story will stay around, until their spirit runs deep in your veins too. Bruce had that effect on us immediately.

We had been staying on and around the coast for quite a while. Jude was pregnant with Miriam and we wanted to have a better birth experience than the big city hospital saga which we went through four years ago when we had Keri. Then, doctors didn't turn up, stitches went septic and unattended, nurses did not wish to touch a patient who had an outside doctor etc.

When we had first arrived to Opotiki we checked out the local hospital and found a maternity wing that was fully stocked and manned and empty! Our baby would have maximum care here, so we were hanging around the area until the baby was born. That's how we got to be there for so long - almost a year to begin with, and then a couple of years off and on after that, meeting up with Bruce many times because he liked this part of the country too.

Each time we met up it was the same routine; Bruce doing much cooking and most of the talking. Sometimes he'd be sick with flu and he'd stay with us eating our food 'til he came right. He became one of our family, like a sort of unpredictable grandfather. When we didn't see him for a while, we'd start to fret until he reappeared. We knew from what he told us that no -one else was looking out for him.

We got to know his movements and planned our journeying to coincide with his. Over the next five or six years we made contact often, shared many experiences together and we saw him go through several changes.

Eventually we moved off the Papamoa-to-East Cape run, went inland for a spell, then up to the Far North. We stayed around the North, ending up on an orchard in Kerikeri. Jude decided to leave bus-life and moved in with a group at Kerikeri who had plans of starting a community. That brought our roving existence to a halt after nearly ten years.

Perhaps ten years was too long a time, but changes are inevitable and I look back on the travelling time as being wonderful days.

I returned to Auckland with the children, moved back into the house we had built before the travelling fever had grabbed hold, and put the bus out the back to pasture.

I had made extensive diary notes of a lot of what Bruce had told me, because at the time of telling they had held great significance to me and I had been enormously impressed with what he had been through. Also, I had wanted time to reflect on many of them.

Now and again whilst on the road I had had guilt feelings about bus-life. Was I depriving my family of a way of life more substantial? Even though we had all agreed to do it together, our larder was always full, and our purse. And even though we all had electric toothbrushes and electric blankets, which ran from the generator. But occasionally the thoughts took hold that the travelling life was perhaps impossible to sustain. Perhaps it was that both Jude and I had been brought up in the city, and you are conditioned that you need a basic minimum to survive.

But then along had come Bruce, with only a bike, and he even wanted to get rid of that. It was an encumbrance, he said, he wanted to get back to legs, which was the way he used to travel. He quoted the Book of Isaiah, in which it says Walk into the Light, and the emphasis was on the walk. And without really saying so directly, he had put the bus into a better perspective for me. What he was saying was you could let go of everything, all the possessions you hold dear and necessary, and still survive. You could get down to just a bike, then even chuck that away and just move on legs. You could still be a rich man.

Three years later after I had made a start to organize material for this book, I went back to look for him. I had a fair idea of where he would be and did find him without too much trouble. First I looked in the secret places I knew he liked, the cubby-holes under the hedges here and there and the off-road hideaways. As I got closer to Opotiki I started asking farmers and fishermen. They pretty well pointed to his whereabouts. In a small community you can't hide as much as you think you can.

I camped beside him for about three days and nights that first time. When I told him I was collating some of the stories he had told me, he thought the whole idea rather unnecessary.

'Mate, do it if you like. It'd most likely be a complete waste of time though. In my life, volumes of books happen to me every hour. And anyway; what's wrong with your life?'

But in the end he warmed to what I was doing, because he felt that many that had met up with him had misconstrued what he had told them over the years, and here was perhaps a chance to set some of the record straight.

It was obvious to me early on that Bruce did have stories to tell. It was equally clear that he was not recording them himself and he wasn't telling them to others either on a regular basis. I became obsessive about getting down accurately what he told me, to the point where I could easily spend all day trying to recall word for word a conversation we had had the night before.

SuperTramp

The story of Bruce is about living in the raw and on the road. And how a self-educated man of lowly beginnings fought the odds so much that the very fighting grew to be a lifestyle. In this country we have no wise pilgrims or elderly prophets. We do, though, have sedentary storytellers, and writers, poets and artists. There has always been in this colonial culture a strong love of stories, due perhaps to the melding together of two major peoples; the Polynesians with their oral traditions and Europeans who were equally verbal. Generations from both cultures in their own and different ways entertained with stories as they spent long lonely periods in their new land.

But Bruce was in a category of his own, closer to the North African wandering holy men, or the sadus of India, with a Zen or Nasrudin quality about him. He was not just a narrator. Indeed, he hardly ever opened his mouth unless provoked. Life on the country back roads of New Zealand had over long years taught him the need to be vigilant and protective.

How wrong one can be by first impressions, and how taking the time to listen can open up windows on other worlds. I once met another man who worked for the council sweeping the streets. He wore unkempt torn clothes and gave you the impression he was one of life's losers. Yet, when I got to know him better, I learned that he was the chief of a very large tribe, a kaumatua, widely respected.

Most of the talking between Bruce and me happened at day's end, on a beach, around a driftwood fire burning deep into the night. There would be just the two of us, under a moonless sky cluttered bright with stars, sparks occasionally darting upwards, with the gentle lapping of waves rolling up the deserted sand. It was a timeless space and a world of peace. Cities, noisy vehicles and hassle, were like some distant planet away.

During the day he had his work and I had mine. He would be off on his bike sometimes, without a word of intention or farewell and not return for a day or two, much like a cat. And too, like a cat, he would not talk much when he returned from where he'd been, yet you knew he had had a full day.

He would never stick to a subject for any length of time when speaking, but would ramble from one thing to another. This was in part a function of the freedom to roam that he enjoyed, but also because his life consisted of patterns that touched many areas at once. Very often he would digress in his telling, so far around that you would think the original thread had been well and truly left behind, and when you least suspected it, the connection came.

I often tried to give him things, to make his life easier. Always he politely refused. Like a spare fishing net I had. No good to him, he said, he was too busy. His day was so full, he would have no time to put it out. Tools, leather-goods, a camera, clothes, all were refused on the grounds that if he needed something he believed it would be provided. By providence.

I even gave him twenty dollars once, to use in an emergency. He took it to appease me, and gave it back to me four years later. He said he'd been carrying it in a safe place 'til he saw me again.

He'd no intention of ever spending it.

'You see,' he said once. 'I've got it *all*, mate. An *over-*sufficiency, in a sense.

I'm a *Super* tramp.'

This then, is Bruce's story, as told by him.

Early Years

"When I was a kid, I used to read about tramps sleepin' under hedges. Ant it used to stick in my mind."

I never got to the South Island, yet my ancestors were pioneers there. They owned one of the biggest stations. At Geraldine it was, near Timaru. They were a big family, thirteen of them. They went right through the Great Depression. The grandparents died and the property was taken over by their lawyer who bought the property himself for about a quarter of its real value. Each child, and one was my mum, got a thousand pounds in cash, plus other incidentals. Then, a shilling in spending power was about ten dollars in today's money. That's about two and a half million dollars for the property. Today that money would scarcely buy a quarter of that area in the same country.

Anyhow I think my mother was somehow cheated out of her share. She took work cleaning boarding houses and in hotels. I have no memories of my father. I was brought up in an orphanage.

I was closest to my sister Pat and my brother Max. Pat went with a foster mother.

She ended up having a better go than we did, in the bloody institutions.

They wouldn't let brothers and sisters be in the same orphanages together in those days. They wouldn't even let us visit each other. That was the hardest, because before I was always looking up to Max, following him around. All I ever wanted was to be where he was. I used to dream of being reunited with him.

My mother would visit but not often enough. Altogether I was brought up in three different orphanages. It was like a prison sentence really, the not knowing if you were ever going to get out. There was no certainty about anything.

I hated school like nothing on this earth. It was foreign to me. And of all the things that I hated in school, arithmetic was it, mate. I wasn't interested in one and one. I hated the sight of it, I thought there was something crook about it and I've been proved right ever since. That's how man can get all his devious ways of finance and put it over the other man. That's also how money-changers work out their interest, how they fleece people.

As a kid I thought that one and one did not equal two. That nothing equalled anything. That no leaf in the world equals another, neither do any two raindrops. The equality system is one of conformity, taking things and people that are naturally not equal and changing them to fit a system.

Arithmetic was going to teach me how to beat myself, and how to put myself in bondage to the money system. All through the teaching of one and one. I knew that and yet I didn't know.

I felt it in me bones, matey.

I knew the answer lay up ahead yet it was right beside me. There were two teachers beside me. Distinctly different. So who is the real teacher? Not the guy you're lookin' at there. The dumbest one is probably the wisest because he instinctively knows already, what the others mightn't learn in their lifetime.

I knew before I knew it. And I knew more'n the rest put together and it was a waste of time listenin' to 'em. An unknown way is better than a known way.

A lot of people seem to spend two thirds of their time dreaming about stuff like the Christmas holidays. Yet when they finally get on holiday, they haven't got time to do any of those things they've been dreamin' about. So they go on dreamin'.

Your dreams are your life. They should be. They should be living dreams. Remember when we went to school and they taught us all about Robinson Crusoe, and all them guys? And I often wondered, because it always appealed to me, and I thought well as soon as I was old enough and free to do anything about it, I'd go cycling.

And I went. Those were youthful days. I'd go and bugger off into the country for a couple of hundred miles somewhere where I'd never been there before and oh it was a great adventure.

I didn't used to have a tent or anything then, I just used to have a blanket and away I went. I was only 13 or 14. I used to go right down to the Desert Rd and all over the bloody place. I don't even remember the snow then. Somehow it didn't affect me.

My eating habits were much different then of course. I didn't ever think strongly about eatin'. But somehow I ate.

It was nothin' for me to go into a butcher's shop and I used to say have you got any spare luncheon sausage? Quite matter-of-factly. And he'd chop off about a third of one.

If I practised that now, it'd still go over, probably. Like the Bible says, whatever ye shall ask, if ye ask in His name, it shall be given to you. Well I wasn't askin' in His name, but I was askin' anyway. I was goin' half the way of the scriptures, and gettin' half the reward, at least. A big lump of luncheon sausage.

I'd go into a baker's and say 'Have you got any spare cakes? Old stale ones, they'll do.'

'Would you eat these?'

'Yeah, sure. Pile 'em on. Got any more?'

Of course, as a boy, people look upon you as bein' different and you could get away with it more that way.

If I was hungry I just pulled into the nearest food shop. Cheek of old Nick, when you come to think of it, and yet it wasn't. It was just doin' the natural thing.

I was like a bird, a bit. Once I had a meal, I was happy. I didn't worry about where the next one was comin' from then. I just went forward, more cycling, camping, down or across any place I could get.

Eventually it'd pall and I'd get a job. I didn't stay long anywhere. If I got a farm job, I'd stay only for the rest of the season and I'd get me cheque and away I'd go. I'd keep on goin' 'til I blew it. I knew that there was another job somewhere down the road. That's what I used to depend on.

One job I remember was working the pump at the Pokeno garage, at the foot of the Bombay Hill. In those days the way north up the hill was a very narrow steep and windy dirt road. Although the garage owner had a Rolls - one of my jobs being to polish the brass around its radiator - most of the cars in those days were Model Ts.

In those days you had to fill a gallon tin from the pump and pour it into the car's tank. There was always a wee bit left in the pump hose, which I put into my own tin out of sight. When it got full I'd sell that petrol from my own tin. Of course the public never knew the difference and I was adding a bit to my wages, see. But I was just a kid, and kids do that sort of thing. That man, was he a crook! He was always bein' called out to rescue some car that was stranded near the top of the hill. The owners would think the hill had done some damage to the motor, and it had stalled. But the Model Ts had a fuel feed at the front of the tank, and if the level got low the fuel didn't reach the engine. All anyone had to do was coast the car back down to the garage and fill up the tank.

But he didn't let on. He told them he'd have to check everything, do an overhaul, and it could wind up costing the car owner a fair whack. In fact that hill was a big earner for him.

His wife ran a tea-rooms there too. She made the most beautiful scones and daily bread. He had a short-wave radio which he'd built and if he wasn't in the garage he was upstairs doing his main aim in life - tryin' to get Russia!

He was a fully qualified engineer though. Sometimes he'd need to make a metal part for an engine and so for a mould he'd go and pinch some of his wife's bread dough when she wasn't lookin'. She'd be screamin' about where her dough had gone while across the yard the whole workshop would be smelling sweet like a bakery.

For many years I did jobs like that, right up 'til the war. I went away with the Second Draft from New Zealand. I volunteered, the biggest mistake you could ever make, mate, you couldn't make a worse one. And I know how to make them.

I ended up in the Middle East, four years and eight months of that. Out of one prison and into another. After eleven years in the orphanage and I'm just starting to enjoy life, then in the bloody army, and I'm being ordered around again.

I think I saw more than my share of action. There was one occasion when the Germans were slinging a lot of anti-tank shells around us. They just consisted of lumps of solid iron. If fired at long range they just bounce around like a cricket ball, zigzagging all over the shop. I saw one come bouncing across the country straight for me so I very wisely thought I'd let it have the bit of ground where I was. Damn me if the devil didn't chase me. I jumped into the air and it skimmed underneath, missing me by inches.

Then the shelling got worse and I finally got hit, funnily enough when I had my strides down and was relieving myself. Caught with my pants down. They carted me off to field hospital with a couple of nice windows in my stomach and a pair of flattened ribs.

On another occasion bombers appeared from out of nowhere and began blasting hell out of our convoy. I counted forty-eight planes. The men jumped off in all directions and started running. For safety I dived under the engine of our truck. I was the only one. The planes swooped low and strafed the men running. There was nowhere to hide behind and they all got picked off. I was the only survivor from our group.

Sometime later I was driving through a small Italian village. I drove across a narrow bridge. Mine was the first truck across. Seconds later a bomb hit the bridge fair and square in the middle, obliterating all trace of it.

Then after a shelling attack near Tripoli I lay for two days in a trench before I was found. Again I was the only survivor in my company.

For a while I was a motorbike scout. We had these big machines that kept cutting out when sand got in the carburettor. Well I thought about it and redesigned mine so the machine could travel upside down and sand still wouldn't enter.

I was in Alamein too. I stood on the hill and watched it all happen below. I knew that this was the pinnacle of man's war development and I thought, what a fantastic sight. There were the tanks stretching out, the planes overhead. There was the enemy coming the other way. I knew there had been nothing quite so fantastic in all of history. This was it! There had been nothing before this to remotely compare and probably would be nothing quite like it again. And the horrors of war at that moment didn't affect me.

Because I had had so many scrapes I felt quite safe at that point, and I stood up even though the shells were whistlin' past my ear. Somehow I knew I wouldn't get hit.

I had bad shell-shock and they sent me back to Britain. We nearly didn't make it. On the way the enemy gave chase. We got strafed and a bomb went right down our funnel and didn't go off - it just stuck there. Everyone was frightened it would explode with the movement of the ship. But it didn't. They tried to defuse it but they couldn't get at it.

Imagine this - the largest ships in the world, mine was the Queen Mary, dotted all over the sea and horizon, steaming so fast over the water to get to Britain that they were almost planning.

I wasn't worried. I felt invincible. After war experiences of being so close to dying so many times, I suppose I lost all fear of death. The Law of Man began to have less interest to me than the Law of God.

We spent a few weeks in Britain doing nothing but drinking in pubs, before being sent back to New Zealand. There was trouble with the authorities virtually from the moment I came back from that war. Because of the shell-shock they wanted me to spend some time havin' psychiatric treatment at the asylum. I told them I wasn't sick. Well, they said, unless I underwent treatment there and then all my pension rights for the rest of my life would be forfeited.

Yeah. Great, wasn't it. I'd just gotten back. Fighting for King and Country, risking my life, and that's all that they could come up with. Well, I still didn't go into that asylum. I'd had enough of orphanages, schools, the army and hospitals to last me my entire life.

I wanted to stay free now, for good.

SuperTramp

Ken Ring

Farewell To The City

"You've got friendly neighbours in the next-building birds, hedgehogs, rabbits, wild cats, the whole blinkin' lot at times, in similar digs."

When I got back to Auckland I found it hard to settle in any one place or job. I knew a fair bit about building and I built a couple of houses single handed.

I bought a piece of land for twenty pounds out at Hillsborough which they had just opened up from being farmland for housing development. The piece that I purchased was near a new house that I was working on already, in Oakdale Rd. When I finished up that I started to build a small house for my mum. At first she didn't want to live way out there. She told me 'I don't want to have to live out in the country!'

One day she said, 'Oh, did you know that your father is buried up there in the cemetery?' Actually I didn't know that because the last thing I knew of him was that he was in Australia. Bit odd really that the place I picked out for Mum was only two or three hundred yards away from her husband's grave.

(The Collins grave is indeed there in the Hillsborough Cemetery in Hillsborough Rd. The headstone reads Richard Collins, died 20th March 1934)

One place I built was two-storeyed, in Milford. I did the whole thing myself, no help whatsoever. I had to carry bricks up the scaffold one at a time. Everybody around laughed. They said I was mad, that it would take me forever. It took ages, but I finished it. Materials were a bit scarce and you had to improvise. I made the bath in that house out of concrete. It was really solid. I bet it's still there.

I moved around at that time, job to job, living in rooming and boarding houses.

I was doing a job for a chap, altering an old house in Avondale. He had struck me as being a decent sort of a fella, and we got along alright. I was living in the house, and he was living there too. We were cutting it up into three flats.

He was an Irishman and very quick-tempered. A young fella, and big. He could thrash out in a second. He could change from a jovial person to a blinkin' ratbag, just like that.

Perhaps if I'd have been a bit more patient and tried to see it his way a little bit more, I wouldn't have done what I did. But I wasn't a patient man any more than he was, and he rubbed me the wrong way often enough to make me just about ropeable.

He did it deliberately once, that was the fifth time I had to take one door out and put it in a different place and then put it back again. And I *said* 'What do you think I am, a blinkin' lunatic or something? Look, I've had that door in there two or three times and every time you've told me to move it over somewhere else or move it back again.'

I said 'Look matey, I'm full of tricks but I'm not a bloody fool altogether. I warned you, if ever you asked me to move that door again, I'm finished with you. You had fair warning. You can stick it and finish your own bloody job. Bugger you. You can't just go on moving a door around forever. Every time you move it you damage the wood, the architrave a little. You can't get it off without doing it. And you expect me to go on using the same material, more damaged, every time I do it, and come up with something good. So go jump.'

Well he landed me one, and he split me blinkin' face. I didn't try to retaliate.

Oh' I said 'that does it mate. You've gone beyond the point where I care to do anymore for *you*. Toodle-oo!

The job was well advanced anyway when I left so it didn't really matter, but at that point I had everything I owned sittin' in his house, all me clothes, tools, everything. I just walked out.

I walked from there to Grafton Bridge in the city. When I got there I thought to myself, where the hell am I going? What for? Where's it going to get me? And I asked myself a lot of straight questions. Like how are you gonna get on for your next meal? I never had a cracker, but he owed me a fiver.

At Grafton Bridge I started sizing the whole situation because I was really on the spot. I'd cut my bridges behind me. There was no going back, not from that point.

I could've still stayed in Auckland but I'd have had to sleep out for a while till I got a bit of money and start from scratch again. But that would've been taking a step backwards, because, I told meself, you'd be no better off than you were at Avondale, you might as well have stayed there.

In fact, I thought, you're not achieving a thing by staying in Auckland. If you move from where you are, you're going forward, going into the unknown, and obviously you're doing something, even if you're only moving.

Also I wondered what I was going to eat that night. And where. I looked down at that moment and noticed the pigeons comin' and goin', scavenging on the path near my feet. I couldn't see any great dinner prospect but they were going hammer and tongs. And I figured that if half a dozen pigeons could find dinner on two feet of bare pavement, then finding food for me shouldn't be too big a hassle either. And that kind of perked something inside me.

I thought *Get up off your arse*. So from sitting on the bench I stood up, and I thought well, I'm going upwards at least. Then I took a step. It was towards Grafton Bridge and I stopped. Nothing special happened. Well what would you expect to happen? Well something did happen and had happened. I'd moved forwards.

In fact I'd gone upwards *and* forwards. Something clicked. Things were getting doubly better already! A feeling of freedom and joy entered my heart that wasn't there before. It all made me realise that I was that closer to Wellington. Why Wellington? Because it's as far as you can get from Auckland, nearly five hundred miles. And things, if not better there, couldn't possibly be any worse. But there was a helluva long way to go. I'd better get crackin'!

Also it was getting near dark and I didn't even know where I was going to sleep that night. I'd really cut my bridges behind me. I didn't even know where I'd get a meal, in fact I didn't get one that night. Also I missed many more too, before I'd gone very far.

But I knew there was no point in going back, I had to keep going forward. I figured I could do this indefinitely providing I could eat just a little along the way. I didn't know how but somehow I felt I would. Although I was a bit hungry most of the time, I don't think that did me too much harm.

But that first day I was quite concerned about where I was going to spend the night. Of more concern was generally what I was going to do, how I was going to live, not so much in a monetary sense, but you can't just do nothing. You've got to be moving somewhere, doing something.

Of course when I moved out of Avondale I left behind my job and the means to do that work, although I wasn't greatly disappointed. There didn't seem to be that much alternative, at that stage. I suppose that was what drove me forward,

Actually, unbeknownst to myself, I was all ready. In a sense, everything but on the road, but I had gone a long way towards it in my general living before I ever set foot on the road. I'd been working unconsciously towards being more separated from money before that.

I knew that money was the key to it all but I didn't know exactly how. The thing that got me on the road was, now I look back, to find *out* how.

To my surprise I didn't get really hungry for quite a few days. When I did, I discovered fruit trees beside the road, quite laden because luckily it was the middle of summer. So I lived off wild fruit for a lot of the way.

Most of what I know now, I learned on that first trip. The things I saw at walking speed, most motorists'd miss. I picked old newspapers out of bins and found that I was only a couple of days behind in the news. People stopped to chat or give me freshly caught fish on the coast.

I was a bit cold at night at times though. So I tried walking at night and sleeping by day, on beaches, anywhere. I tried walking fast at night to get warm, then laying down and sleeping 'til the cold woke me up and then continuing for about another hour or so and then havin' another lot. But travelling at night made it hard to see to find food and much less enjoyable.

On that first trip I never spent a cracker except for one thing. I picked up sixpence as I was going out of Gisborne towards Wairoa. The last shop I got to in the main street on the left hand side as you're going towards Wairoa I found the coin outside on the footpath, and I bought an ice-cream and I reached above my head.

There's a big peach tree there and it was loaded with peaches. I thought, well, I've got the ice-cream, that'll be cream so I might as well have the peaches with it so I could have peaches and cream.

Now this tree was hanging over the footpath loaded with big golden peaches and in the window I was looking at peaches that were for sale in the shop. I saw a big car pull up in front of that window and a very large woman got out. She took a sniff at the window and into the shop she went. She came out with a bag full of these peaches. She left the car door open, put one foot on the curb and she was sitting there munching these bloody peaches, but while she was doin' it I was reaching up and getting mine down for nothing.

That gave me great joy. I thought, well here I've got it all, mate, the best things in life are free. I was milking the tree as fast as I could and out came the blinkin' shopkeeper. He had his apron on and everything and he said 'By crickey, you're havin' a lot of fun aren't you!

I said 'I sure am mate, I'm enjoyin' it. These ice-creams are good but the peaches are even better 'round here!'

'Aw,' he said, 'help yourself. Which way're you going?'

I said, 'Eventually I hope to end up in Wellington.'

He said 'Take some with you, all the best.'

There was that woman sittin' there still, munching her tatty old peaches and here was I having a great old picnic.

I can remember being up at Cape Runaway on that first trip from Auckland, having nothin' but a shirt, a beret and a pair of sandals and pants. That's all I left Auckland with. Not a damn thing else. And at last I'd reached the Cape. I'd had a few fairly cold nights on the way down and I was getting about piddled off with that aspect of things and thought I'd better start thinkin' seriously of a way 'round it.

I started figuring things out and decided that you could make a kind of a blanket out of grass quickly if you went the right way about it - you could even make a mattress out of it too. But the one thing I didn't figure was that you'd have to do it by lights, and there were no candles around. How're you gonna do it?

I said, well, you'll just have to knock off an hour or two earlier and prepare in daylight. I figured that the daylight hours were made for seeing in and your tasks should be arranged accordingly and if you run out of light, don't worry. Wait. There'll be a whole new lot tomorrow.

That was one lesson that stuck with me, because from then on, my day started at sunrise and finished at sunset. Everything was completed by sundown.

On the way on my first real trip I hardly bothered with shelter at all. I just lay down in long grass. The night wind would blow right over me, sometimes there was rain with it and often I'd stay dry.

The worst condition was when the rain was beltin' straight down. Now what do you cover yourself with? I found black plastic was no good or for that matter any waterproof, so-called, stuff, because humidity builds up underneath and condensation starts runnin' everywhere and drippin' on you and you're wet through in no time. You turn slightly to let it all out and hey presto you let in some rain. Just what you don't want.

Then I made this discovery. You can use water to fight water. I found a sack, a tight weave flour sack, the old heavy variety. It was lying across a ditch in a howling blinkin' gale. Well it was lying in such a way that there was a gap underneath, and I went to pick it up and something made me stop and look. When I did I noticed that the grass was still fairly dry underneath. You see, the sack, he soaks up water and holds it. But only so much. The water makes the material swell and get fairly water resistant to any more.

So I instantly knew what to do.

After that if it rained, I put newspaper down first on the grass. Then I'd go and soak two sacks in a stream, wring them out, put one inside the other and use them damp as a top blanket. You might think that's pretty fantastic mate but it'll keep you dry.

There's an opposite, too. On a dry night of course you don't have to worry about a waterproof top part. But if you think the weather'll be cold, and you can tell this by any bluish haze on the horizon, then you need warmth underneath you. You need to prevent against your cooling down. Go around reaping green grass, pullin' the stuff out by hand but it must be green. Don't pull it from where you're going to actually lay. Pile it there and spread it a bit and lay on it while your blood is still warm, soon after you've been chasin' around. That'll stay warm all night. The green stuff is moisture-laden. It's like each leaf is a miniature hot water bottle. And your body on it keeps the heat in.

Or you can dig two trenches, one for the bed and one for cooking, make two fires and sleep in one when it's died down enough. You chuck away the ashes but the ground's warm and stays that way.

If it's a hot night and you want a cool bed, reap dry grass, not green. and just lay on that. Dry grass lets air come and go between it and your body.

To begin with, I used to dig holes for my hips in the ground when I made my bed but after a while I stopped doin' it because my hips grew accustomed to the hardness of the ground and grew hard themselves. Generally if it was rocky I wriggled around 'til I found a place where my hip'd go between them.

Once I had a day of real bad squalls, driving rain and wind. Then a spell of fine weather followed in about an hour by another blinkin' lot. It was in a piece of open flat country near Foxton, and I was getting the full force of this bloody racket. I decided this is not for me. I could be doing it a lot better, if I sheltered, for a start. Then I thought well how the hell're you goin' to shelter way out here? There's not a bus-stop or anything else, to get behind.

I don't know why but I absent-mindedly put my hand in my hip pocket and I found I had this bit of double-o-two plastic. It's the very thin stuff and very light. And I was toying with the idea of pegging it down and making a kind of shelter from the wind and rain.

I attempted it but it got ripped away from the pegs - it really gets torn around, that stuff, in the wind, and so light. So I thought, what a bloody dead loss that lot is. While I was doin' it my eye caught sight of the boundary fence that runs alongside the road. I started to put me thinkin' cap on.

Well, I reckoned, the world is your enemy. It's rather like fighting fire with fire and water with water. In the first case you can stop any fire by lighting another fire in front of it and allowing the two to come together. When they come together at one point they go out. Now how do I fight wind with wind? Use the wind and make it my ally.

I thought about it with my back to the wind. I could see that this was more comfortable than the wind hitting my front. You're an automatic wind-breaker. I tried to peg the plastic to the fence but the wind just ripped it off. The wind was coming sideways across the paddock, through the fence to me.

Then it occurred to me to put the plastic on the inside of the fence and the wind might hold it there. Peg it for me.

That's it!

Wind fighting wind. Sit in the lee of it and the storm'll go right over you. And the more it blows and the harder it rains the better!

So I sat in the front of it and I got me coffee out and I brewed up. I made a loaf of bread.

Now, I wondered, what am I going to do if the wind starts blowin' the other way? I can't hop into the paddock because I'll be trespassing. I must stay on my side of the road. Well, I thought, I could cross the road and put the plastic on the other fence.

Okay, that covers east and west winds but what about north and south? Directly in front of me is only road, no fence. What if the wind comes straight up the road? At that point I decided I would have to get on my feet and run..

Why? Because it's faster than walking.

Because I'd be going somewhere as fast as I could.

Because I'd be looking for a bend in the road!

Now there's all directions covered and you've always got shelter no matter where you are, and from something that you can carry in your hip-pocket. You can use it as a cover for a bed-roll, a bath, hand-basin or sink. There's a million different uses.

Fantastically light thing, so small, not much bigger than a cigarette box when it's all folded up. Yet it's eight foot by eight foot. Soft too, when you sit on it, you wouldn't even know it was there.

If you can use nature, of course that's the best to get a similar result. For instance, a hedge in a hollow, if it's not too damp, can be a real place of pleasure, mate. Snug, warm and sheltered, it's hidden from the public gaze. You can create as many rooms as you like by flattening areas with your body.

This little plan will give you built-in alarm clocks as well. The sweetest and the best. Birds and cicadas.

Just before Opotiki on that first trip I saw a sign that said this way through the gorge to Gisborne or that way around the East Cape to Gisborne. And I asked a motorist 'Is this the way to Wellington?'

'Aw, go the gorge way', he said, 'it's at least a hundred miles quicker. Take that road!'

So I thanked him and headed off the other way.

'Thanks', I said 'I'm in no hurry, in fact the longer the better!'

I wasn't all that much wiser than when I left. Somehow I'd eaten because I wasn't dead yet but I'd dropped a lot of weight. It took about three weeks. And I'd at last reached the Cape. I had got by. I was damned cold sometimes though.

One episode I remember, I was goin' forward down the road and it was nearly time to think about turnin' in, so I started castin' my eyes around for a likely place to camp down. There were two sides of the road and big borders and a lot of rough edges. I thought oh well, there'll be no hassle, but then a bale of hay appeared, lyin' on the road. I suppose it dropped off a farm vehicle. By crikey, I thought, this'll make a nice bed. I didn't wish to drag it too far so I went to the side of the road with it. What did I find?

A hollow. Just exactly there.

Like a saucer.

So I just tipped the bale in, pulled off the wires around it and then broke it up and tousled it. When it packed down a bit, my feet were straight. I had a small bag of clothes, that was me pillow, I put a blanket on the bottom and then the blanket up over the plastic bag with all me clothes in it. What a beautiful soft springy bed.

Later I thought, if I'd've cooked me meal first and then put the bed down, the ground would've stayed warm like an electric blanket. But as it was it wasn't cold. All the wind blew right over.

I often use that method at a beach.

Sometimes I'm hungry and cold. It's sometimes hard to find good shelter. So what I used to do was dig *two* holes.

One was the kitchen. Light the fire in one and pile it all with driftwood. I only went near it when the embers were smouldering. The hole was only deep enough so that when you sat down the wind went over you.

Then I had the big sheet of plastic. I put a centre pole a couple of feet long in the middle, stretched it over the top and put a bit of driftwood there to hold it.

When I got to Wellington though, I was certainly in good shape. In and around the city I still slept in the long grass. I mucked about there for a while and then I got a job with the railway at Cloburn. I was looking after the grounds at this hostel. The meals were sumptuous and you had your own hut. We ate like fighting cocks, three or four choices of meat, cakes and even three or four choices of blinkin' soup. The chefs had those high hats on. Well, you wouldn't have thought we were workers, more like princes or something.

Talk about going from the sublime to the ridiculous.

I had struck out for Wellington first because that was the end of the line. No other reason. But when you get there, it's not, it's only halfway. But you must go that way. south, to go north. So every two and a half months I did a circuit of the North Island. Continually. I went around the island so much I was gettin' dizzy!

So much so that one fellow said to me one day over near Tirau, by the service station that's beside where the winding hill starts towards Hamilton and Cambridge, 'hey, you're hanging 'round here a lot!'

I said 'What the hell are you talkin' about?'

He said 'You're only here a few days ago'.

I said 'Don't be bloody silly. It was two and a half months since I was here and I know that because I've done a complete circuit of the North Island on foot. That's how long it takes me. So I know I wasn't here yesterday or the day before that or the day before that or the week before that. You're dead wrong mate. You'll have to take my word for it.'

He said 'You won't want to be seen around here much more or people'll begin to get suspicious about you.'

SuperTramp

I said 'I don't give a bugger about what they do. I wouldn't be doin' it if I did. I believe this is still a democracy here and I've got a right to move freely. Higher men in higher places than you have tried to convince me before you that I shouldn't be doin' what I'm doin' but until I'm convinced, I'll be doin' it that way. So far I'm not convinced, far from it. You're going to see me often, matey, *be prepared for it!'*

Ken Ring

Camping Days

"Another fella said once 'I always see ya walkin' I said 'Oh, I'm doin' many things.' 'Yeah,' he said, 'but you seem to be all over the place.' 'Well,' I said, 'I don't have to stop where there's a camping ground, or a shower, or a telephone.'"

In Wellington I thought I'd get me a job to get some cash and buy real good camping gear, the best. And I did. I really stocked up. And I found under test conditions none of it stood up. In about a fortnight I'd chucked it all away, bit by bit.

I gradually found myself not trusting any gear that was bought or someone else had made. The demands I put things to hadn't been heard of before in camping circles. So I'd buy a thing as it was and then change it to what I thought it should be.

The yankee backpack was useless, it made you walk with your nose near the blinkin' footpath all the time and the tent was a waste of time putting up. The sleeping bag when it got wet weighed about a ton. You could hardly carry it around. So I threw it away.

But I picked the wrong time to throw it. That night it was dry weather, and I froze!

There was a time soon after the war when I used to go here and there, change my job and everything that went with it, and I remember walking the streets often, looking for boarding houses. Now it was the same with the camping stuff. I was looking for the perfect system and that was a mistake. Now I don't look for anything. I wait 'til it comes. Might take me a while sometimes but I just go in the fresh air until something happens.

I spent a night in Waiouru once, but never again. Oho, gee, it was cold. And I was under some trees too. And it was snowing. Oh God it was cold! It was such a hell of a way to the next place, Taihape, and there was so much snow on the road, I could hardly move. In fact from the very next day I was completely stuck for a week.

I went up the road a bit and came to this little wee place, it had just a railway station and a little wee store. Maori name but I forget what it was. The blinkin' snow was deep. I went into this empty railway house and was sittin' there tryin' to light a fire. Lo and behold, who should walk in the door but a cop.

I said out aloud 'I've seen it all now.' Out the back of nowhere, trouble with the law. What in hell are you doin' out there in that?'

'No', he says, 'what are you doin' here?'

I said 'Right now I'm enjoyin' a nice big fire. With *sleepers!*'

He said 'You shouldn't be here.'

I said 'Yeah. I should. And by the law too, matey. I happen to know the survival laws and under certain circumstances you can take over any shelter, anywhere, as long as it's not being used. Well if this is not a survival course I'd like to see one!'

He said 'Oh, that's alright then. Move out as soon as it starts to thaw or you'll be getting me into trouble.'

That's the one time I got clear, just by a little thing I learnt not so long before. I was talkin' to a bloke and he told me about it. Apparently the law takes second place in a case like that. If you can see a shed anywhere, even somebody's wash-house, you can move in. But only while the emergency is on and it runs its course. Then you have to get out.

I had another instance of this just out of Opotiki. I was camping under some trees, eucalyptus, and there was this empty house just across the road in a paddock. I slept outside there just one night, with one eye on the house. The next morning, I heard the fire-engine coming. I thought what's the fire-engine doin' way out here? Bloody hell!

They were coming to burn that house down. Yeah.

They thought I was going to live in it.

Well even if you did, was it any skin off their noses?

Anyway they treated it as a fire exercise, bloody firemen all over the place. All over it like a lot of blinkin' ants and they were tryin' to control the fire in a lot of different ways. They were lighting fires around it all the time and runnin' around it with hoses and puttin' them out again. That just taught me how stupid they can be, like a lot of bloody kids - dinkum!

SuperTramp

Your bed is never the same twice on the road. I've slept on boulders. And you couldn't put your hip between them, they were so thick. And yet you spent all night tryin' to. So you turned on the other side and you got that one a bit sorer too. Well you lasted out 'til morning with two very sore hips.

But there was some good in it. You woke up with a new spirit. You hadn't slept and you were superman that day. You took off like a bomb. You couldn't put enough space between you and that bed quickly enough to forget all about it! Unless you be there again tonight!

When I woke up one morning I heard PWAH! PWAH! I thought what the bloody hell's that? There's no trains out here! You know what it was? A bloody hunting dog, panting. Suddenly a shotgun was just about up my nose.

'God you're lucky' this guy says. 'What the hell're you doin' there?'

I said,' Well crikey, surely I don't have to answer that one, mate. You can see what I'm doin'.

He said, 'You're takin' a risk. I could've let you have both barrels.'

'Well,' I said, 'you might've done me a service mate.' Maybe for a quick exit. Not that I'm the most unhappy man in the world by any means, nevertheless, I believe there's some good in everything, even that!'

He said, 'Let me get this straight. You wouldn't mind?'

I said, 'Look I'm not askin' you to shoot me, but if it happened it happened.'

'Don't you think,' he says, 'that you might be takin' a helluva risk, sleepin' in places like that?'

I said, 'No. To me, life is fifty-fifty. It's just as likely that I'll be shot as it is that I won't be.'

He said 'I thought you were a bloody duck or something. What told me not to fire was the dog. He didn't point like he usually does when he spots a bird. He just kept runnin' around in circles. So I thought well there can't be a bird there, something else. I jerried to the idea that something unusual was around, warranting further investigation. You happened to be it!'

Quite honestly you never knew what was going to happen next. I had a guy actually firing at me once too. Down near Foxton. I was sleeping next to a hedge, right on the side of the road, and the next morning there was a fellow out shooting with a shotgun. He wasn't too far off, either. He let go - bang, bang.

I heard zing zing of the bloody things flying and ricocheting around me. I knew he was pretty close but I couldn't see him. I thought I'd better stay where I was and not move and see what happens. He came ambling by on the other side of the hedge. He was on his own property but I was on mine too, so there wasn't much he could do.

I said 'Are you enjoyin' your shootin' mate?'

I thought there was just the odd chance that word might've got round that I was happening along and they would've liked to scare me out of the neighbourhood. I wanted to disappoint them.

I said 'That was an expensive duck, two shots and nothing! You must be a bad shot. You'll have to do better than that next time matey.'

I'd set off up the East Coast, find myself a place near the sea and nice surroundings and plenty of tea-tree that I could clear me a box-shaped space - that was my walls, and I then just used to put the tarpaulin over the top.

A canvas tarpaulin by the way, is the same as an old sack in terms of dispelling water - works the same only it's bigger and a lighter material. But I didn't have a canvas one. At that stage I only carried the sacks because that's what I put the bottles in by day, and myself in by night. And for an overhead cover I joined some together. Sideways, the tea-tree stopped the wind and everything.

On the other side of Te Kaha I made my first semi-permanent camp. That was where I put in my first garden. It was one camp that I never got pushed out of.

I moved out of there in the end, of my own accord. It had started to get winter and I thought, aw, the fishing's finished now, it's all just kahawai surf-casting stuff at the river mouth, a bit of a hassle.

It wasn't a good place to be in the winter, not many possibilities for food. Anyway I used to spend most of my winters moving. You had a better chance of getting food that way because you were coming onto something all the time. But you had to keep moving.

At one time I got in the habit of travelling at night, especially when the weather was cold. There were less cars on the road and when I started picking up bottles, the moonlight picked out the bottles by shining on them. So did the car lights.

That's the time I discovered libraries. You can look up books there and I used to try to identify plants I had tasted and that hadn't affected me in any bad way. Often they fitted into families of known vegetables. Certain wild grasses are like wheat and all that.

Then after reading and taking notes I'd sit in the nice soft chairs and fall asleep. You can sleep all day there and no one says boo but if you sleep out at night on a park bench or a hundred other places they bring hell down on you.

Silly isn't it, when you think of it. You're only layin' down your head, wherever you are and whenever.

Like in the bible, Jesus himself never ever suggested that you or I should ever sleep. No, he always said rise up. He said rest, which was a trance state, more beneficial than any sleep; it's when you can be in a kind of sleep with your eyes wide open. It's rest.

They didn't have beds in the biblical days but then you don't need a bed to sleep. You can sleep on top of a blinkin' lamp-post mate.

Man doesn't understand the hidden power he has, regarding sleep. He can go for days and days without sleep. Sleep is rather like a meal. We eat too much, too often, because we become accustomed to it. That's the only reason. I believe we can go many days without both and be better for it.

For a long time I had the idea of using a beach umbrella as a tent, for sleeping legitimately under. I couldn't see any reason why it couldn't work. And it turned out to be bloody fantastic, a real good shelter. You've got to have one with a vinyl top though. It'll turn any water away and it's strong too.

The one I eventually got cost me twenty four dollars, brand new. Later I made an adaptation by fixing a skirt right round out of plastic so it was like a wall about eighteen inches high. There was a doorway and I could peg the sides into the ground in a high wind.

But I never knew the true value of it 'til I came to use it and realise how it gave me loopholes in the law.

It made life a lot easier for me because I could use it in lots of places where you could never put up a tent. I mean, even in a park I could put that up, because it's quite commonplace to see people sitting under beach umbrellas in a park. There I wasn't doin' anything unusual so there were less complaints. Only when I did it at night, and someone happened by, then they would think it was unusual.

Sometimes I didn't put the umbrella up at all. I just had it beside me and slept beside the bike. Just in case it rained, then I'd put it up in seconds. On the beach I'd put it up, put me bed down, hop in and stick me feet out the end of the bed. Then in the morning I just folded it down, rolled my bedroll up and away I'd be, within minutes. Sometimes I wouldn't even have breakfast.

The biggest umbrella I had was an eight footer, six foot across.

I had ten people in it once. One day going toward Tauranga I saw a road I never noticed before. It looked most inviting, tree-lined, tar-sealed. Oh, I thought, there must be something good down there. I felt like a little boy, my heart was racin' with excitement.

I started to pitch my camp in this beautiful spot on a bend under some trees. Then suddenly I heard a yell. And all of a sudden, out of nowhere, to spoil the whole scene came a crowd of boy scouts. Here was me trying to set up camp, and think of this, that and the other of what to do next and they're jabberin' at me at the tops of their voices. Crikey, you've no idea the row it was.

Number one said 'How do you eat? Er, where do you get your food?'

'Oh,' I said, 'the birds feed me. The bird, he gets up in the morning, he takes off, the first thing he thinks of is something to eat. And what he eats generally has seeds in it. When he goes to the toilet, he drops that seed as well, and the seed comes up and I walk along later and find my vegetables growing beside the road.'

Oh boy was I gettin' a great kick out of seein' the amazement on those faces!

Number two - 'Where's your fire? How d'ya cook?'

'On the kerosene cooker,' I said.

'Where's your flour?'

'There's ten pound of it on my pannier. There's also ten pound of sugar. And as well there's herbs and milk powder. I can make bread, stew, soup and ginger pudding.'

Of course they wanted to see it. It was all possible, but it amazed them.

Number three: 'How do you get over hills?'

'I don't think about it, but when I'm over them I thank God. I think of life, breeze, all sorts of things. When you know there's a hill in front, then you also know there's a reward on the other side. It's the downhill. So you push twice as hard just the one way, so's you earn it quicker. You think of the blessing you're coming to.'

Others, later, would say to me, 'are you going up that hill?

'Aw, it's in front of me, isn't it? Eh?'

'Do you think you can get over?'

I'd say, 'I don't even think about it. I haven't yet thought about it. I'll think about it when I'm over.'

Anyhow in the end I had ten boy scouts all sitting under my umbrella tent, all with their feet toward the centre-pole and their backs to the wall.

I made a lot of camps at Hicks Bay through the years and used the beach umbrella for several seasons.

Once there was an almighty hell of a storm. The main brunt of the bad weather only lasted about four hours but trees were uplifted like someone tearing grass. The only building there, a church, got picked up whole and blown away. Phttt! Just like that! There wasn't a tree left standing upright, bar one, around me. It was uncanny and the wind kept up for hours, as if all the Maori women in New Zealand were whining at a funeral. It sort of got into your blood.

What saved me was the only tree that didn't get blown over. And somehow or other I had chosen to stick my umbrella next to it before the storm began. It was a pohutukawa and it had planted itself three times. Three times branches hung down and re-entered the ground. It was in the process of jumping over the road to plant itself a fourth time. One day cars are going to have to drive underneath.

Well I camped on the leeside of that during this howling gale with nothing but my umbrella between me and the weather, while the storm cut great paths through the forest. The vinyl was flapping like mad and the ribs were goin' up and down and I had to hang on to the ribs to keep them down. Otherwise the whole thing would've taken off.

But it held, but it was that tree that kept me fairly dry and safe. The umbrella wasn't the same after that. The ribs had weakened with the movement and started to snap, one by one each time I unfolded it and put it up. And I couldn't afford to buy another umbrella, so I had to turn to other systems.

Once I built a log cabin at Hicks Bay. I carried the logs one by one out of the river. It was beautiful when it was finished. I had a lounge and a bedroom and a kitchen and a veranda. A Maori chap with a Scottish name used to come by; he owned a great big homestead further up the valley, but he'd spend all day with me, yakking. He hardly ever went home.

In the end I got pushed out of there by the health department. There was another Maori family living in some tent or other on the beach, and the department told them to move.

'Well,' they had said, 'what about that pakeha up there in the cabin?' So I was ordered out, no other reason.

Kid number four said to me 'Where do you get money?'

I said 'Matey, from so many places, it'd take me more than two minutes to tell ya.' He felt robbed.

Number five whispered 'I bet he sells bottles.'

Well, that made me think all night. That's what we did as kids. How come we forgot? And that's what gave me the idea for bottles, that occasion and that kid whisperin' it.

So the idea for my livelihood came from my very opposition - the boy scouts!.

The Bottles

"I doubt if I'd go back to the bottles now. It's a dead duck mate. There's been a lot of fellas doin' it down through the years. As a matter of fact it's quite revealin', really, that's an episode all of its own, quite another story from the road. Yet you could write volumes about it. A bottle is more than most people think it is, I can promise you."

When I first got going in a big way on the bottles, after the boy scout episode, it was on my way north for probably about the third or fourth time from Wellington. And I soon got to know the ins and outs of the whole business.

There are certain banks and ditches'll give good yields. The shape of the road and the size of the undergrowth have a lot to do with it. There's rest areas, lookout points and sloping banks a mile or two either side of a shop, for a start.

There are certain places where I'd always find a bottle, and some places where I'd never find one.

For instance there's the intersection, the cross-road and the side road entrance. People stop to read the blinkin' sign, and whenever they stop they start eatin'. And hitch hikers get out to change cars and dump stuff while they're waitin' for the next ride. The bottle is often the first thing they discard.

A bend in the road is good pickings. Probably passengers in the front seat throw stuff out their window when they think the oncoming cars can't see them. And just over a hill is good for the same reason, only now it's so that cars *followin'* can't see what's goin' on.

All this could be in the remotest country, where you'd never think, to look at it, there'd be a bottle anywhere for miles, 'til you go and look under the blackberry.

Now walkin's the best, because you've got to be travelling slowly to spot them. I used to walk thirty miles a day. I had my bedroll down my back, Aussie-style, on a diagonal with one end over one shoulder and the other under my armpit on the other side. My clothes were wrapped in my blankets and the lot was covered with polythene and rolled watertight. Both ends were joined with a short length of rope across my front. It was an even load and I could walk upright.

Over my shoulder was a sack with my daily needs and the bottles that I found each day. I called that my picnic bag.

I always felt sorry when I had to stop because it would be past dark and I couldn't see any bottles. And I was losing good territory. I was passin' it over.

You can get more bottles in half an hour walking, than you will even riding a bike in half a day. That's how many you can miss. Your feet roll on them when you're walking on the long grass. It's a lot of fun, mind you, damn good.

I used to enjoy it, because each bottle has a character of its own. You got to know them. They became my friends, especially broken ones.

Some well-meaning person would pick up a bottle they'd see on or near the road, they'd pick it up and put it on some cocky's boundary fence. When you happened along, you'd see it. For two or three times when you came that way you'd be fooled by that broken bottle because from the road they looked whole.

So you gave them all names so you wouldn't forget them. It could get quite personal. I used to call one Charlie and one Jim and *Oh gee, it's you, you bloody bastard!* You could get quite attached to them.

Some bottles, I hated to part with them. Isn't it funny, nothin' special about them, just ordinary lemonade and that. I don't know if it was how or where I found them that did it, but I found there were a lot of spiritual things about it, too. I became more observant, you had to be in the first place to actually find them.

Then you began to look deeper. *Last time I came this way, Billy, you were the other way round. Er, what's the caper?*

He'd turned himself around and he'd be pointing north instead of south. And I wanted to know why.

So I turned him south and took a note of it. I came along again and he was facing north again.

Who was doing it or what, I don't know. It seems fantastic but I say it was spirits, having a bit of fun. And how they contact you is by putting bottles in odd places where they shouldn't be.

Some Maoris around here must reckon the bottles are theirs. They came up to me once and said 'Hey, we seen you pickin' up bottles!'

'That's right,' I said.

'Well they're our bottles, you know.'

'Well,' I said, 'why aren't ya pickin' them up? When are ya gonna start? '

'When we're ready, eh'

'Okay, but if you're not careful I'm goin' to end up with all your share and mine too. I don't know which is which. Pick 'em up mate. Don't leave 'em there on our land.'

'But it's our land.'

'Okay,' I said, 'These are yours? Even though I picked them up, you have 'em. I'll dump the lot by your door. And then you can dish 'em out to your mates, those that think the bottles are theirs.'

And I did just that. I took them two big sacks full and tipped them all on the grass. Of course I didn't try cleaning them up. They weren't mine to do that.

When he said 'ours', I took personal offense to that. But I've nothing against the Maori people or anyone else. Sometimes people don't even know in themselves what they are saying.

So I regarded it as a message from some higher force and I stopped picking up bottles then, and said *It's all yours mate, you can have them. I'll find another way!* But I had placed a wrong interpretation on what he said.

When I realised this I also realised the spirits'd do anything to get me to go back on the road again. Sometimes I'd be cycling along and I wasn't having a particularly good day; of course this was them, they were switchin' the bottles and hidin' them as I went past, and all this.

How I knew it was so true was I got a dollar's worth of bottles per day as regular as clockwork. Now why wasn't it more variable?

Yes I could go three parts of the day and only have half a dozen bottles. You could take nothing for granted, but something averaged out. When you left in the morning you never knew how long it was goin' to take you to get your quota. It could take you all day to pick up fifty bottles. You could pick them all in half a day, some days. You could take all day to pick them all up and not pick one up before lunchtime, and half the day's gone. You'd say *'Doesn't look good, does it?'*, yet you always got home with your dollars' worth. Because they all come thick and fast in the last two minutes.

Yeah, all of a sudden they'd be rollin' in, just nicely in time for me to do all me baking and get into bed before dark. Of course a day consisted also of fishing and everything else besides bottles. But when I realised it was part of the bigger picture I started up again.

I picked up milk bottles too. They were great, double in value to everything else. But I stuck strictly to a code. Only the ones that were thrown out or dumped. I got about one in twenty-five, which was five or six in a week. But they were certainly worth findin'. Five milk bottles gave you a dollar.

Ordinarily to do that money you had to produce eleven big drink bottles and one small, to say nothing of the difference in bulk and weight and everything else. Also with the bigger spout they were the easiest ones to clean. In every sense it was a better lark. Less hassles too because with them there'd be no labels. I was startin' to learn the finer points of this business!

Sometimes you struck trouble from certain shopkeepers as far as giving you the money for them was concerned.

A grocer at Te Aroha was inclined to knock you back a bit.

He said to me, 'Oh, I don't take those kind.'

I said 'Why?'

He said, 'Well, I don't sell those kind of drinks.' And in his fridge there, were those very drinks. So he didn't sell 'em eh?

I pointed to them and said, 'How come, mate?'

'Aw,' he said, 'this is just the tail end of the last order.'

I said 'Yeah? Well the next time I come into this shop I never expect to see that drink again.'

I expected that what they told me was the truth. And I made it my business to drop in if I was passing and take them to task. They probably did not have a legal binding, although that technically speaking was debatable, but I thought they certainly had a moral obligation to pay four cents on every small bottle, eight cents on every big bottle, for every bottle that anybody, Tom, Dick or Harry, could bring in. Providing one thing: that they did sell that particular brand. Of course he sold that brand, but he didn't want to shell out to me.

So I said to this same grocer 'Look, as from now, the moment that you decided that you were no longer gonna pay back the deposit on those bottles to the bearer, you break contract with the bottle company and the public. You are an accomplice to the crime of failure to fulfil the terms of contract as promised in writing on the bottle.'

I tried to keep it above board because occasionally I'd buy a drink and just chuck the bottle away myself.

Just as a matter of principle.

At Te Puke I used to strike trouble, although he took a lot of bottles at first. It wasn't the bloke himself, but one of his daughters behind the counter.

She said to me 'That one's got a moth in it. Eeeeoooh! A moth!'

I said 'Are y' sure?'

'Yeah. Eeeeoooh! Yucky moth!'

I said 'Look. Come over here lady.' I pulled one out of her stand that looked grubby on the outside. Full of lemon juice too.

I said 'I dunno where you got that one from. But it looks like it came out of someone's cow yard! I think I just about *recognise* that bottle. I picked that one up myself, not so long ago. Eeew! Isn't it *dirty*!' I made sure they all heard it too. The boss came out of the shop, so I did another *'Ew'*.

I said 'This one. In your stand. Man, do you mean to tell me you'd sell that?'

I said 'You're worse'n I am. Mine's only got a moth in it. Yours has got plain dirt on it. And that's being mild about it'.

He couldn't deny it because there it was in front of him.

I picked up every and any bottle I saw, and I had to bend me back to pick it up. I considered that that was labour. Well, aren't I entitled to be paid for my labour? So I went to all kinds of lengths to see to it that any bottle I picked up went in another direction. So that I got paid for it.

Some of them originally had painted trademarks instead of stick-on labels. If they were weathered very badly, this paint got discoloured a dirty black. When I put them on the counter I used to turn them towards me.

They'd say 'The man on the truck says he's not takin' any more dirty ones,'

I said 'They'd only be a bit dirty on the outside though. And anyway the bottle company has got washing facilities. Look in your fridge. What do you see? Here's Coke, Fanta, all the rest of it. And you notice something. Every bottle is clean, inside and out except for the liquid. So whatever was on the outside of these bottles has been washed off. I've never yet seen the soft-drink liquid put on the outside of the glass. I doubt if I ever will. So why should my bottle which is unavoidably discoloured only on the outside, affect the inside drink?'

It's rather like puttin' in good clean seed in the garden. And you expect good clean vegetables. But you don't get 'em. You get a helluva lot of weeds. And you have to pull 'em out for nothing. I wasn't havin' that situation, not with bottles. I wasn't doin' anything for nothing. I was getting little enough as it was.

At one shop the fella wouldn't do any business with me whatsoever; wouldn't even look at the bottles I had in the bag.

'No, he said, 'I can't go payin' for bottles just now.'

'Why not? I said.

'Cause I'm a little short, at present.'

'Crikey,' I said *you're* short. What d'ya think I am? If you're short compared to me, that's *short*, mate!'

But what was happening was this, and I didn't find out 'til a long time after. If the grocer or dairy owner didn't make sure that every bottle was in a reasonable condition, then they'd get the same bottles back in the next consignment of lemon drink. So their trade dropped away because people kept seein' dirty old bottles.

So they started making all kind of excuses so they wouldn't have to take my bottles, 'cause they thought that a good percentage of the dirty ones was coming from me.

I did my best to see that they were in a reasonable condition but I wasn't goin' to cut my own throat. So I thought, well I'll compromise. I'll make the bottle as near to perfect as I can. I'll scrub it with a wire brush. And I did. I did all that was in my power to clean that bottle. So particular that I even used detergent.

Homemade.

Most of my bottles, considering the numbers I was handling, in the time available to me, I sent back pretty clean because I made a personal rule that every bottle had to be handled a minimum of three times. One of them took me the best part of a day, to get chewing gum out of it. Some had drinking straws forced in and stuck. They're a hell of a job gettin' out.

Dead mice even. Oh man, what you couldn't find in a bottle! I got more than my share of *them* out. But one or two shouldn't hurt anybody, let alone the occasional moth.

I remember saying to that grocer 'Look mate, you must have moths in your bloody shop. That guy just got in there. I just put my bottle down on the counter. Are we going to have a hassle now about whose moth it is?'

From that day on at Te Puke I wasn't quite as popular again. But before that we got on alright.

So he was a bloody fool to himself. He could've said to me, *Look matey, the pressure's on!* And told me why, and what's goin' on. I'd've listened. I couldn't make them any cleaner, that's for sure, but I could've given him a few less dirty ones. They had to be gotten rid of.

Even though it was my own choice of employment, somebody had to do it.

Aw, some of them took it in great spirit. Some thanked me very much and said *I think you're doin' a great job.* Others were downright rude, and they hated your guts. But generally I'm happy to say that disposing of the bottles was, at least, acceptable. In any business you have to take a few insults. You're a public servant in a sense, because you're serving the public.

Up at Katikati, oh gee, you ask that guy if you ever go in his shop - did you ever know that guy with the bike, that used to pick up bottles - Man, you won't have to say another thing' and you'll get my reputation, right between the eyes! I gave him bloody millions of bottles. And he took it all in good heart too, I'll say that for him.

Mind you, I built a lot of trade for 'im too, the bottles he handled was a bonus for him. Even if he did have to put up with a little bit of poop now and then from the suppliers. Well I had to put up with my share of poop too. It all went around in a circle and everybody got their share!

Some whole towns wouldn't take any bottles at all. In Foxton for example. There, they have their own brand of drinks, they have their own factories that make these drinks; all drinks have Foxton written on them and they tell you quite point-blank *That's a foreigner. Sorry, but we don't accept foreigners. Anything outside of Foxton doesn't count.*

I knew every type of bottle, all the hassles connected with the different types, exactly the boundary line along the road where you had to stop pickin' up that particular bottle. Because beyond that point you're carryin' it for nothing. *That's a Wellington bottle, that's a foreigner! Dead loss. We don't take that.*

I still used to make heaps of 'em, at different points along, so I'd save time on the way back down, next time I did a down trip. So I'd go to known heaps instead of pickin' all day. That way I worked a bit in bulk handling.

So there were quite a few ins and outs. It was quite a business, quite a fantastic business. Very original yet so workable.

I wouldn't like to count 'em mate, how many I sold throughout the North Island, or to count the miles I walked, just picking them up. They're countless. Yet now looking back, I can almost feel like I never travelled a mile.

I used to keep a tally at one stage. I gave it up when I realised there was a pattern and an average God had in store for me. I can remember one day twenty-eight large and sixty-two small.

Not a bad day's pickin'.

Working

"It makes no difference what time I wake up and get out, the birds are all up before me. They're getting breakfast, fussing, spring-cleaning and runnin' errands while I'm still tryin' to open the other eye. And they're finished and havin' smoko while I stumble around bleary-eyed. There's a lesson in that."

People have said to me 'Wouldn't you like to have money?'

I'd say 'What for?'

'Oh, you could go for a trip somewhere.'

'Well', I'd say, 'I've been! And that was all for nothing, too! I don't need to make a lot of money just to go for a trip.'

Then they'd say 'Do you ever work?

I'd go 'Yeah. Every day. Never miss. I bet I'm up before you in the morning!'

'Oh yeah, but what I mean is, have you got a job?'

I'd say 'Yeah. A dozen jobs. I'm just gettin' ready to cook the breakfast now. That's the first one!' Knock the wind out of their bloody sails for them.

'But where do you get your money?'

'Oh,' I says, 'somehow or other it has a way of comin', if it comes at all. I'm not worried. I get by. But why money? Why didn't you say something else? Like where do I get my blinkin' hat? Well I'll tell you *that* one. Down the road, mate. Off the road. That's where I got it. '

'Yeah but don't you ever work?'

'Well I just told you. I'm cookin' breakfast.'

People say to me 'How can you do it? To think, when there's all those people in Opotiki workin' every day, and you're out here sunning yourself and fishing.'

I says 'How can I do it? Piece of cake. Because I'm fishing, and that's working.'

The Lord thinks so too, I'm sure of lt. Otherwise I wouldn't get any fish. There's very few days out of the three hundred and sixty five that I don't. He sees to that. And I do my bit. I ride out here and I ride back. I fish, pull out all the stops. That's work. If I was mendin' me pants it's still work.

Of course they only see it the money way. That's their god.

I could never get used to going to work, working for a boss every day. But in fact I do just that, sometimes fourteen hours a day just for the love of it. I think it's beneath a man's dignity to have to go and ask another man for a job. You shouldn't have to ask anyone for anything.

Back in the city, it seemed to me to be a big hassle to get money for rent if you had to work to get the money; and to get the work you had to be in a dirty stinkin' old factory or something.

It didn't seem right to me, I think a nice day is made for you. If you don't use it you're depriving yourself just for the sake of a dollar or two; you're depriving yourself of some of the best and most beneficial things in life, snubbing God in a sense.

So I thought it better to settle for a different arrangement, whereas you had a great big beach umbrella and that was a factory you worked in, and when it was shiny you let it down. Then you worked in the sun. When it rained you just put her up again. So a situation similar to that I would call a compromise and I would be prepared to co-operate on that basis.

But I didn't see the sense of being behind four walls and under a roof on a beautiful day when I could be under a beautiful tree, not forgoing anything of the things I like; that is me tucker and a good rest, a bit of work, hunting - even if it's only for bottles!

This appeals to me. It didn't always appeal on a wet day though. When it got wet for maybe a week, I'd stick up me tent, make meself comfortable, sit, switch on the radio and enjoy it, 'til it blew over.

We have such potential within ourselves; our brain is such a fantastic thing. Just that in itself makes life endless. The potentials within ourselves to make life within ourselves is fantastic.

You're never goin' to run out of a job. For as long as I live, for ever, I'll never be without a job. Because I don't call a job money, or wages. Within an hour I can have two or three fish caught, if I want, and cooking merrily.

If you can' t find a job in the worldly sense then the best thing to do is to start lookin'. Only this time look a bit harder than last time. You might find that nothing you do stems the idea that you're an unemployed person. There are some very tired, sick, and on occasion perhaps, lazy people. But they're all workin', in spite of themselves, in one way or another.

And you don't have to be on your feet to be workin', it can be on the bones of your arse. Your brain could be workin' flat on your back! Just thinkin' is work.

Thinkin' what you do is sometimes harder work than the actual doing of a thing. Perhaps you're immobilised, in a hospital or something like that, but you don't have to be absolutely like a cabbage. You can be doing constructive work, work that if you were on your feet you wouldn't have time to do in that manner. To all intents and purposes, anybody coming into that room could say 'by crikey, he looks ill; or lazy', and yet you could be deep in thought.

They think that if you're movin' your limbs you're workin', otherwise you're not. But for all they know you could be appreciating your surroundings intensely. By moving your head only slightly you could see a whole lot of new stuff. So it was well worth the effort, wasn't it! You could've been hard at *leisure*.

There's nothing like a bit of solace. If shutting yourself off from the world is not the biggest job there is, I don't know what else is. It is certainly not being unemployed.

And you don't have to live other people's lives or use their ideas. You can look for your own. It's easy to create your own work. I'm glad to do it.

An electrician said to me one day 'Where's your apprentices?' He'd set himself up as a God.

I said 'Matey, 'I'm only an apprentice *meself*. And I'll never *know*, so there'll never be any apprentices but myself. How about you?'

'Aw', he said, 'I've got five or six there.'

I said 'Poor fellas. With all due respect, did y'ever see it any other way?'

He said 'Wouldn't you like to draw a payroll?'

I said 'No mate, I'd rather have my dignity, thank you.'

I once went for a job at a big building firm in Auckland. Old Vic Pollard, he says to me, 'You seem to fit the bill, I think you'd suit us alright. When can you start?'

I said 'Oh, about the middle of next week. Be alright?'

He said 'Yeah.'

I said 'Just one thing I haven't mentioned - I haven't got a toolkit. Are you still interested?'

'Oh,' he said, 'let's think. That's a little bit unorthodox you know. But I'll tell you what I'll do. Back in my early days I used to work in a little workshop here as a joiner and I've still got all those tools tucked away in my basement somewhere. I'll dig them out and you can have them.'

See how easy it is.

For years I lugged my bloody kit everywhere around. It palled. I just woke up to the fact that there's easier ways of doin' things. If they want you they'll do anything for you, if you'll let them. If you don't let 'em, they won't.

He came to me the day I started, and said 'You know, I think you're somethin' special.' But without actually sayin' it of course. 'And you're gonna have special treatment.'

He said 'Look, you don't take any notice of anything anybody says in this place. Nobody can give you an order. You can choose your own timber from any pile you see, the best to the worst, it's all yours matey. If you want anything, come and see me.'

So I owned the joint. The whole timber company. Like a prince or a king, virtually.

I've often wondered about it since. They didn't really know me from a bar of soap, nor did they really know if I could prove my worth when they hired me.

If it was me I wouldn't operate that way. I'd say 'No set of tools? Well you're not much good to me.' But from that job on I've never bought a tool. Yet I've never been without work. I've had to turn it away.

However I could go around any town any day of the week and

if I did nothing else I believe I could pick up enough money on the streets to keep me going, without any other source of income. I know I'm riding over it every day on the bike. I can't even be bothered getting off to pick it up if there's no necessity to.

Money is just like bottles. There's certain places that I know for sure that I'll find some before I even get there. Also there are certain times. In the city I used to look for money in the streets by walking into the rising sun first thing in the morning. The reflection of the light on the silver'd catch my eye.

You wouldn't think that timing had anything to do with the picking up of a coin. Anywhere in the city where people use loose change - bus stops, telephone booths, parking meters, is where you go. But in the country it's quite different. Just like finding bottles, you must work out where the most likely places and times are.

But isn't it the same for everything? In the middle of winter you'd be wasting your time looking for rabbits, 'cause there aren't any rabbits around. In the breeding season, look for one and you'd have a better show of finding some. This is timing. If there was a desert on your left and a mountain of gold on your right, you wouldn't go into the desert to grub gold.

When there are lots of holiday-makers around, there's lots of loose change. When it drops they're too proud or in too big a hurry to pick it up. So the more people there are around and the more hassled they are, as they are in crowds, then the more money you're going to find.

I had plenty of tricks and favourite spots. I could go for a ride to Point Chevalier, enjoying every minute of it, and come back rich.

On the way I'd go past Chamberlain Golf Course, where they parked their cars. Always good pickings there. People are in a hurry to get out and play. And when they're waiting for a bus, they can't find their loose change quickly enough. Some goes on the ground and they haven't time to bend over and get it or the bus'll leave without them.

Another thing too. It rolls along and goes into all kinds of funny places. You learn too that even though you've found only one coin, it could be only one out of a dozen that rolled out of his pocket when he pulled out his hanky to blow his nose. Push anything to the limit and you'll find nine times out of ten there's always more. That's the rolling kind of money.

If a note fell from someone's pocket, where would it end up? The wind might take it, or the rain. If you glance your eye over all the rubbish, leaves and things banked up near a storm water drain after a storm, you could find a note or two. But it'd be a bonus, and that's the way you should look at it.

I used to use these dried milk tins as billies, and to find one in good condition, nice and clean and just been dumped was like finding a jewel for me on the road. It was a real find and it really meant something because your life depended on these things that gave you that little bit of extra comfort.

I reckon your reward comes as a result of what you can do,

how you live and that sort of thing, and your work is included in that.

You are a member of a family, this family is the family of God, and he regulates your income. This isn't just money but also food and clothing; he dishes it out and he gives you according to how he sees your heart and how it is set. If he knows that you are quite content to be happy with a little, he rations you to that extent. Now and again he'll do something very special for you, some little windfall will arrive, quite unexpected.

You might pick up a dollar note. It could happen. Even way out in the country.

For a start I used to think somebody had seen me goin' past and they were hoppin' out of the car and plantin' 'em, but they could never happen to be in that same place all the time way out in the wops. And who's gonna run miles from home just to put a dollar note there? It's just a little extra for me and I could say I could take it a little easier today, that's two dollars in two day's work, so I can spend one day havin' a bit of a rest, just once in a while.

If it was ten dollars, I'd have several days off and go fishing. If I knew I was goin' to have a good long holiday up the coast, I'd add part of my dollar a day from the bottles onto that. When I had twenty dollars I'd have up to three months holiday. Well some people couldn't even have one meal on that.

(I said to Bruce 'I'll make you a wallet if you like, and I'll make it to your specifications.' I thought he wouldn't need what I made regularly for sale to the craft shops - complicated and multi-pocketed. I said 'If I was to make you one, what kind of compartments would you prefer?'

'Aw', he said, 'Well I'll have one pocket for my addresses, one for my cheques, um... one for the twenties, one for the tens, another for fives; then I'd need space to put me small change.... and then another part to put letters in..'

I never did get around to making it).

You can find all sorts of other things besides money layin' on or near the road. If I find say, a right shoe, that fits me, I simply wait until I find its mate. Eventually I do. Sometimes I find another right one. Well then you looked at both closely and kept the best one and threw the other one back where it came from. Because now you'd been given a choice. If you got a better one it was certainly worth bendin' your back. And the next time you find one, the odds will be better now that you'll get a left one.

Once I found a diver's wet-suit lying in a ditch. It looked brand new. What occurred to me first was that this was the ideal thing to wear instead of winter underwear. So I held it against me but it was far too big. And I thought it's far too good to consider cutting it up for fire-starters. So I put it on the bike and went on, in this case up this great hill.

At the top there was this car parked and a man in it. He spotted my bundle.

'Where'ya goin' diving?' he asked, because there was no water for about ten miles.

When I told him how I came by it he said 'Will you sell it to me?'

Now this put me in a difficult position.

I don't like being any sort of a trader and I would've given it to him only I'd just walked up that long hill without findin' a single bottle. And I felt that there were at least freight charges to consider, from the ditch where I picked it up, to here.

So I said 'How does two dollars sound?' I knew it was worth well over thirty.

'It's not enough,' he said.

'Now look mate,' I said, 'I hate seein' somethin' not bein' used. I'll probably stash this and never use it but I would have to live with the knowledge that somewhere there would be you wantin' to use it and not bein' able to. Also, if I charged you any more I would be makin' a killing out of what is just a piece of good luck. That should never be the way of things. Good luck should be shared, like good wine. Two dollars gets us both off the hook. Take it!'

He took it alright and he took off quickly too, like a madman, in a cloud of dust.

I have stashed stuff all around the country that I can call on if ever I need it. It's buried at the foot of trees, in banks and things. Sometimes in plastic bags or boxes. I've tools, spanners I've found but can't carry with me, stuff like that.

SuperTramp

There's a whole bike I found near Taupo, and there's a whole bag of salt down the coast that probably fell off a truck.

Sometimes you find things that are obviously stashed already by burglars, like a whole set of golf clubs and a trundler, brand new, near Levin, and a new lawnmower engine still in its box near Matata and a box of sealed headlamps, still packaged. Well I don't touch that stuff, you know, I've no need for it and anyway it's no business of mine.

Now where would you go if you wanted wire and solder for something? Walk along the road looking at lamp-posts until you see one that looks either new or worked on recently. And you can tell that by the remains of smoko rubbish such as cigarette boxes or patches of thermite ash. At the base of the post or nearby, and you might have to scout around a bit, you'll find wire and hunks of solder, just thrown in rolls.

I got a chair for nothin' from a second-hand shop by just tellin' them that I wanted it.

I said 'Have you got an old chair 'round the place that needs repairin'? I'll repair it myself. One that you could give away I mean. One that's not worth you repairin'?

So the guy says 'Go out the back there and have a look and see what you can find.'

I'd already looked matey, and I knew what was there. I went straight to it and I brought it out and I plonked it down in front of the counter and I said 'This'll suit me admirably. Just what I need.

It'd fit my camp-rig to a tee. It couldn't be more better for the job! I reckon this'd suit me the best! It just wants some needle-work, some finesse, here and there, stuff that a lot of people mightn't be prepared to do.'

'Alright,' he says, 'you can have it.'

There's a lesson here: you can always get something for nothing, always. When you do a deal, keep your eyes and wits about you. If you get your eyes screwed on something, don't be satisfied 'til you've got it. For nothing.

You can shell out, but the more you do, the more you'll have to. If you don't put up opposition to people who want money out of you, they're only going to think that you're a bigger fool ever than you were before.

Why not turn it around a bit and get somethin' out of them, to balance the budget?

People claim that I don't pay rates and I don't pay taxes. Well, I tell them I do. I pay about three thousand dollars a bloody year. That's the super that I don't pick up. I qualify for it. It's a gift to the government. I let 'em have that.

Once I went to the tip to get some plastic to keep the frost from some early plantings in a garden I'd started. I found some and some geezer strolls over and says 'What're ya goin' to do with that?'

'Obviously,' I says, 'what d'ya think I'm doin'? I'm puttin' it on the *bike* matey.'

'Oh you can't take it outa here!'

'Well that's what I'm goin' to do.'

He mumbled 'Silly bastard. You're not supposed to take anythin' from here unless you ask first.'

I said 'Who did you ask when you took stuff from here? I seen you takin' piles of bloody stuff.'

He said 'Oh, I'm allowed to.'

I said 'Are you any better than I am?'

'I have a higher authority,' he said.

'Well in that case, *so do I!*'

He was takin' stuff by the truckload himself. And if necessary I was prepared to assert my equal right with him.

'Now, if you want to get your superiors I'll decide how to deal with them.'

There was about a dozen television sets at that tip. and someone had put the axe through all the tubes, to make them valueless. But they were trade-ins, and the cabinets were perfect. All the electrical components, resistors and all kinds of blinkin' things were there, must've been worth dollars. Even speakers. All a man had to do was gather the lot up, take 'em home, unsolder all the components, and sell them to the television repair people at a low price; which would've amounted to a lot of money. Especially the speakers.

But he drove the bulldozer over 'em and buried 'em.

I said 'The trouble with you matey, is that you'd rather see good usable stuff buried.'

He said 'Oh,' I don't want to bury it, but I've got no choice. It's got to be buried. It's in the road.'

I said 'It wouldn't be in the road if someone took it away.'

The value of a thing is not what it is, is made of, or cost. A thing's true value is its use that you can put it to, nothing more or less. A bit of plastic from the tip that to the person throwin' it away was rubbish, to you can save you a whole crop of spuds. Just because it'll keep away the frost.

The thing to develop is not the art of payin' cheques, but the art of not payin' 'em. Gettin' somethin' for nothing always pays off. No holds barred either, except pinchin'.

You can be real nasty to a joker and he can be lappin' it up, if you go the right way about it. When I was building, and a carpenter, I used to put in big orders for timber. Then's the time to chuck in extras. I used to see some bits of broken wallboard.

'Aw,' I'd say, 'that's not much good to ya.' I didn't ask him if I could have it because if I did he'd have said no. So I just repeated 'that's not much good to you mate. It's broken! Nobody's gonna buy that!'

'Oh,' he says, 'they might. Sometimes they buy bits.'

I'd say 'Ach! You don't mean to tell me you'd sell that. A big firm like this? Nah, you're jokin'...'

'Aw,' he'd say, 'take it away! And shut up!'

Then I'd say 'There's a broken bag of cement in that shed there. It's gonna make a hell of a mess if it gets tipped over or anything. I'll take it away for you for free, mate. I guess I could find a use for it, at a pinch. Anyway, it's no good to you, is it? Big firm like you? And we do a bit of business too, here at times, don't we? We get along well.'

'Oh take it away!'

You have to lay it on them.

Ken Ring

Waiheke Island

"I'd like to see a few more trapseyin' along. I'd like to see a few more bikes behind me and all doin' the same thing too. But they're not there. That disappoints me a little."

I'd like to see more bikes but I can't make 'em be there. I can only tell 'em what Christ could only tell 'em, that I can't make 'em do it. They have to do it themselves. If they won't do it, if they're comfortable in what they're already doin', then they've got somethin' to lose if they change. Still, there's always a better meal down the road as far as I'm concerned.

I only came across one person about my age, livin' a similar lifestyle. But he wasn't a regular. He used to call into the orchards around Napier and Gisborne and places like that, and he used to get apple-picking in season and get by on that. But he liked his bottle, his spirits.

He was always happy and cheery, a bit of a roughie like meself, but he liked to do things in a more sophisticated kind of a way.

As a matter of fact I employed him on a job I was doing for a builder. Les was his name and he came from the Jersey Islands. He skipped ship years ago and the cops'd been on him for years tryin' to deport him but somehow or other he managed to skip it all the time.

For him things could get rough at times and tough because he couldn't get work from the same sources because people wouldn't have him on, once they found out that he didn't have a regular country. Anyway even if he did have a job he couldn't stay long 'cause the cops'd catch up with him.

When he came to me for a job I could see that something was wrong. I knew that he was hiding from something so I said 'Look mate, I'm a bit of a roughie meself and I know very well that there's something with you. I'd like to know what it is, not because it's going to make any difference whatsoever but because I'll know what answers to give when I'm questioned. So let's get our heads together . What's the story?'

He said 'Well, I skipped ship and they've been on me ever since. I'm only just managing to keep them off. It goes a little while then they're back on the job again.'

'Oh,' I said, 'that's nothin' as far as I'm concerned, that's your pigeon. If they come on the job and pick you up, I'll shake your hand and say goodbye. All the best. I wouldn't be able to do anything for you in that respect. But you've got a job for as long as you want to stay as far as I'm concerned, here. I won't be payin' your wages. I'm just a sort of foreman. I run the job. You won't be asked to do anything I can't do myself anyway but you'll have to measure up.'

Well, talk about work. He was a great little toiler. Gee, he toiled. And he turned out to be quite a good guy. Well, he was the only one I ever come across. And I never even cycled with him, though he always had his bike.

I did meet up with him once on the road, way out in the blue somewhere. He was coming from Wellington and I was going the other way. He was the only other thing on the road for miles, besides myself. He had his bike and gear there and when he saw my gear - 'Crikey Dick, where did you get that thing? What've you got on there?' He had just scratch gear. A canvas bag with just one or two things.

I said 'Aw, matey, this is the way to do it. I could put me bed right down in this spot, and be as comfortable as if I was in anybody's home. I'm ready for any emergency like that. I don't have to rush anywhere; it's here. I can survive, oh, a couple of months, without taking on any more, without moving another inch. It means it sets me free from hotels or rooming houses or rent and money and everything, because my transport is free. I can move when I feel like it, or I can stay at home when I feel like it. There's rations, sufficient flour and tea.'

He was a bit floored by my sophistication.

The last time I saw him was on Waiheke. He'd been havin' it

pretty rough I think. He was dealing in uncustomed radios and things and getting a bit of liquor money that way. He was in a nervous state.

He was down at the Auckland wharves, just where the ferryboat leaves. At that time I was staying on the island, and he was standin' there.

I said 'Hey mate! By gee! How ya goin' Les? I haven't seen you for bloody donkeys' years!'

'No,' he said. 'I've been hearin' that you were here there and everywhere but you was always just a jump ahead of me. Now you've nailed me. Somethin' was tellin' me to contact you.'

'Well,' I says, 'you've come to the right guy. What's the story?'

He says 'Well, I haven't anywhere to stay. I haven't got any money either.'

'Aw,' I said, 'if that's all your problem is you can share my palace (my beach umbrella, though I didn't tell him that 'til we got there). Mate, I've really got it good now. You've never lived in style like this in all your life!'

Of course he perked up. I could tell he was interested.

So we got a ticket for him to go over to Waiheke.

Then we were standing on Onetangi Beach (good fishing there mate, fantastic, certain place that only I know, aw, half a dozen snapper there within an hour no trouble).

We walked in the gate of a house.

I said 'Here it is mate.'

There was a widow living there but she was in Auckland. She only went there for the holidays. And she gave me permission to stay in the orchards in the back. I got myself all set up nicely and everything. Plenty of fruit. It was summertime.

I said 'What could you hope for nicer, matey?' I didn't say anything about the beach umbrella. I said 'Well, this is it. This is home.' We went up the steps and went straight to the back yard.

He said 'Where's the toilet?'

I said 'It's out the back there matey, you just go over there.'

He said 'Mind if I go in the house and have a wash?'

I said 'Oh, you don't wash in *there*. There's the tap there at the back, that hose-tap.'

'Eh?'

'Yeah,' I said. 'You're not livin' in there. You can do better than *that* matey. Come on with me. This is where you'll be livin'.'

He said 'Eh? There? Where do you live?'

I said 'There. Your room's the one on the right! Turn left when you get to the end of the passage and you'll be in your bedroom. Strictly right where that centre-pole is, is the end of your half, matey, no more and no less. And you'll find out that if you put your big toe out too far, it's likely to get wet sometimes!'

Oh but he was happy. Because just down the road was the Onetangi Hotel and he got down there and got himself a bottle of gin - that kept him warm. I fed him and he got used to it after a while: he was alright.

SuperTramp

But I had a bit of a tiff with the old girl, she came out one weekend. She told me to get down the road. I think she got a bit bitchy you know, on heat, and she fancied me to do something about it, I don't know, but it was no dice. She just got unmanageable. So we moved out.

I was goin' down the road, up towards the ferry. Old Les was trapseyin' along. Havin' to move at short notice set me back a bit: I didn't want to move all me gear, get on the boat, and go back to that lousy city and then maybe go room-hunting for Les when I got there; it didn't appeal one iota.

But little beknown to me, just up the road was salvation. I heard 'Hey!! Ooh!!

There was an old sheila comin' down the road.

'Just the fella I want to see! Put it there! Put it there! How are ya mate!' And she grabbed hold of my bloody hand and shook hell out of it.

What a welcome I got, right there on the road, crikey dick, the heads must've stuck out of all the windows in the district. She had yelled it out. 'Put it there!! So I had to put it there and by gee did she wring it too. And I'd never seen her in my life before.

I said 'I'm a little mystified. Why the welcome? What's it all about?'

'Aw,' she said, 'I've been hearin' all about you. You know Mrs Watson'

I said 'Yeah. Been stayin' at her place. I know her very well. I've just left her! So Mrs Watson and I aren't talking anymore!'

'What's the trouble? You've left her? You're leavin' the island?'

I said 'Yes, but not willingly. She decided, at short notice, that I've overstayed my leave. I'd've liked a little longer here because I was just gettin' used to the place.

'Oh,' she said. 'I've got a place just up here. You go up to the store up there on the hill, by the grocery on the left-hand side of Onetangi road. You go up there, make yourself comfortable, you'll see the bach at the back. Put all your gear in, make the bed, there's clean sheets, everything's there. You're *home*!'

Anyway, it turned out that her name was Mrs Wells and she used to be an old trammie conductor during the war years and just after. She was a hail-fellow-well-met sort of type, a real hard shot. Man, did she have the answers. She liked the bottle, too, and of course this suited Les down to the ground!

Before the night was out we found ourselves in a nice comfortable bach, free rent, *if you see anythin' needs doin' 'round the place just do it*, no questions asked, a bit of tucker, a little toddy to go to bed, our washin' done and a blinkin' drink at night - well, could you ask for much more?

Les had one bunk and I had the other. She was getting about ten dollars a week in the season for that bach but there was nobody there because it was just past the season, all the people had gone back to work.

'I can't let it anyway, now,' she said, 'so it might as well be lived in. You can do a few odd jobs to offset the tucker bill and everyone'll be happy.'

She turned out to be a great old girl, bloody marvellous. She made a great cobber for old Les. I'm not a big drinker myself but not a wowser either. But she was just his type. She had a cobber about three hundred yards down the road called Mrs Gotobed, and the pair of them often gave overnight board to down-and-outers, it turned out, or people they met in the hotel who drank away their money for accommodation.

Where Les got the money from, God only knows, probably off her, but he bought a ticket.

'Come with me,' he says, 'we'll go into town on the ferry; I've got a surprise for you.'

When we got there he says 'Come up to the Princes Wharf,' so away we go.

We had some cakes and that and he said 'Well, so long mate, thanks for all you've done for me, I wish you were coming with me, maybe you will later, maybe some time I'll shout ya. But I'm on my way to Aussie!'

Yeah, just like that.

I said 'Where's your bike?' (Because he had one too).

'Oh,' he said, 'I took it up the gangway, it's somewhere up there. They don't charge you if you do it that way.'

'But where the hell did you put it?'

But he was an old seaman. They only had to know that and they do anything for him. I don't really know if he ever even had a ticket. He might've been workin' his passage, in a sense.

But I haven't seen nor heard of old Les since those Waiheke days; he's probably still in Aussie. And I think that's how he used to exist. They wouldn't give him a permit to stay in any country so he just used to jump ship, stay until the pressure was really on, then stow away again somewhere else, running a shuttle between here and Australia.

I haven't been back to Waiheke since then either. I'd dearly love to have met Mrs Wells again. If you met her you'd meet a character, would you what! A real hard shot, a real experience. If you mention me you'd have a greater one, I promise you.

She was taken with my *'menagerie'* as she used to call it. There was my pussy and fully laden bike, all go. All systems were go. I was way ahead of the times.

She had a great depth of heart. I'll say one thing for her that I can't say for any other woman I ever met mate, we never crossed swords. She was too matter-of-fact, happy-go-lucky, too well-oriented to get into an argument with.

I don't even know if she's still alive. She might've sold out or got out, been pushed out or carried out for all I know.

Letters to me are unreal. Too distant. I like things real. If a person's worth knowing he'll visit or I'll drop in on him. So I don't bother writin'. But that doesn't mean that I'm tryin' to take it away from someone who does like it that way.

Mrs Wells was the only person I ever wrote to. I felt I owed her something, but I couldn't give her anything really. I gave her something that was priceless anyway. I wrote her one letter that I knew would especially appeal to her.

About a year later I was pickin' up bottles between Tuakau and Pukekohe, way up in the back, and under a hedge I found an old Christmas card. That was the only paper I could find to write to her on. On one side was the usual Christmas verse and somebody had written underneath that:

'To Aunt Molly, from Dot.'

So on the other I wrote

To dear Mrs Wells. Between you and I we've found a friend; the person who made this possible, who discarded this Christmas card. This makes it priceless. This card brings together the four of us in true Christmas spirit. I'm sure they won't mind and I'm sure you'll understand.

And I said something else. *Don't on any account ever discard this letter. It's absolutely <u>priceless</u>*

I knew she'd see the joke in that because it'd cost me nothing! I'd picked it up off the road. I knew it would appeal.

Well, I thought I'd post it at Pokeno. When I got to the post office I slapped the money down. The lady said 'What's that for?'

I said 'The stamp.'

She said 'That's not even half enough! You've got to find more!'

I didn't know it had gone up. All I had was the money it took to send something donkeys' years ago.

Then she looked at me and smiled and said '..oh well...put that one on it!' She gave me a stamp and I put it on and the whole thing disappeared into the mailbag.

I don't even know if Mrs Wells ever received it. If she did, no doubt she put it up on her mantelpiece. But all my time on the road, I struck very few like her, so spontaneous and when I met her, solving all my problems so quickly. A very happy type and regular as clockwork. Come five o'clock and down to the pub she went, whether she was by herself or not.

She always respected my opinion on things and she never put herself out of line with the liquor, although she came home happy once or twice.

SuperTramp

Ken Ring

Animals

"My cat was eatin' tapioca once and I said 'Hey, do you know what you're eatin'? Frogs' legs!' He looked up without battin' an eye and said 'I'll take it.' God done a wonderful thing when he sent my cat along."

Every bird that arrives is a friend. Every dog, every cat, every person, every bug is a friend. It can be something to look at and reason about and perhaps something a little comical. It could be actin' in such a queer way and doin' funny things that you can't help laughin'. A friend, sent for a purpose - it could be walkin' up your leg! And you might be tryin' to flick him off and you do, but he'll be back for another go.

This is all to draw you out of yourself, and so ease the pain. There's always somethin' to either pester you or do somethin' to annoy you one way or another or be just a plain bore, askin' stupid questions. An enemy yet a friend.

They suffer the same pains, they get sick occasionally, they go through all the trials and temptations that you do, there's damn little difference and yet so small, so similar, so full of spirit and joy and happiness but in comparison with you so ill equipped to deal with situations like that, yet so unafraid.

A man once said to me 'Why don't you get a horse?' And what I told him was that I wouldn't enslave an animal. I give them the same freedom I want other creatures on this earth to give me. And I think horses know it.

Every time I go past Omaio there's a field there with some horses and they canter over to say hello. They know, and they wish me well.

One day a mare come over with her foal to show it off to me and say 'Isn't she the prettiest thing you ever saw?' I always chat back now to her, if I'm passing, hello and how're goin' and that. And I know if I was to enslave a horse *she* would get to hear about it. And she in particular, would be upset.

By Te Kaha the sheep'd come down a track beside my camp every morning. Every day at the same time. They'd say baa baa, gidday or something and I yell out hi fellas, see you later. And in the evening they're back and it's did you have a good day?

I believe the Almighty made Man in a variety of ways and that is what the world of animals is part of. You can see human-looking faces on them. And always gentle and peace-loving, like children who haven't learnt to hate yet.

When you look at one dog you see them all, and I believe you can give a message to one dog for another dog and somehow that message will get delivered. If a dog you know has died, you can still talk to him, through the living ones.

Animals are just like people, only better.

Watch the birds, they'll teach you a lot. A fantail has his beat, like a policeman. His hospitality is enormous. If you wander into his area he'll jump up and down, here and there, over and under, showing off. He'll talk, he'll chatter, he'll sing in his heart. And he'll escort you to the edge of his beat like an old friend seein' you to the door.

Sometimes his mate from the next-door territory will take over and you get the whole blinkin' routine again.

Birds love life. They sing in merriment in the sunshine to express their joy. I've never heard a dog bark all day just because the sun was shining on him.

Some funny things happen out there. Once I was fishing with a hand line. I'd caught nothing for hours. I didn't know whether to give up or persevere. Then a finch suddenly appeared and landed on me line. He put his beak around it and pulled as if to pull the line in. So I took that as a sign to stop fishin'.

I went back to me camp and that bird trailed me, a short distance behind. I made pancakes and fed him too. And that night it blew a storm and the bird got under my tarpaulin. He saved me from wastin' any more time in useless fishin' and I probably saved his life.

Even the seagulls play tricks on you. For a long time they used to have me on, stabbing at your bait and at your gear, makin' you think that they're gonna pinch it. But it's just kids' stuff. They're only having fun.

Actually they're doing you a favour. So long as you don't leave your lunch out in the open. Anything else, they're only there to help you.

They never drive the fish away. They know when the fish are there and that you've a good chance of catching one. And there's an equally good chance that a head or a gut will come their way. This is good for you too, because the offal brings flies. So the flying things are there to clean up the garbage for you for nothing.

The seagulls think I'm an enigma. They know I'm an original and that I do catch the fish. You go down there and look for where the seagulls are, there you'll find me. There's not many about in the off season, but those that are here are around me.

One in particular, he's always there. Trying to tell me a certain message. I think it was Jonathan Livingstone Seagull himself. He was a certain colour, with a black beak. He'd stand there by the bloody hour and every now and then he'd go over to my bait or my gear and he'd start looking for something to eat, apparently, but he wasn't really.

But I thought he was a pincher. So I began to shoo him off. Then I realised he was just taking stabs at things. And it was clear that he was trying to create the illusion and kid me into thinkin' he was after me bait.

In actual fact the message he was tryin' to give me was, surely matey, by now you know that I've never yet taken anything off you. I'm here to guard your bait. When the other seagulls came around he'd shoo them off with that wild cry noise. He was doing me a guard duty.

To most people he'd be just a thief, but if you take the trouble to look, you can discover more. If you look for good you'll find good and if you look for hidden messages you'll find 'em. Anyway I threw him a head now and again, so he got paid.

Some guy said to me, 'Don't you regard fishing as killing?'

'What is killing?' I said to him. 'How many ants did you stand on. on your way to this place in the last hour?' For no good reason whatsoever, not even to get a meal. How many living things do you stand on, crush under your feet? Is that killing?

Yes. But I wouldn't kill needlessly. I wouldn't go out and shoot a great big deer, just to take a steak off it and leave the rest there. I couldn't handle that. I don't pick unnecessary vegetables either that I can't eat immediately unless it's for convenience, to save myself a huge hike every couple of days to where they're growing.

Motorists kill for me, I don't have to kill for my meat supply. I've had possum, hare, rabbit, pheasant, duck, pukeko, hawk, all off the road, freshly killed. The meat might be pushed over a little, but it's perfectly alright.

If there's a lot of possums in a particular area I walk up the road about half a mile away from my campsite then half a mile the other way. I take note what is on the road. In the morning I do it again and so I know which meat is freshly killed.

So why kill when it's done for me?

Hawks also sometimes kill for me. If I see one swoop down below a hill I've managed at the odd time to run up and scare him off. I've had a few rabbits that way.

I don't believe in ownership anymore. I find it more beneficial not to own things but to use them. You own a dog and what d'ya have to do? Put that dog in bondage. You have to put a collar around his neck and keep 'im tied up for life. Purely because out of your own folly and you said you owned him.

But the inspector came 'round and said 'You know you have to keep your dog licensed.'

I said 'Whose dog did you say? Yours? Did you say yours? You're being a little presumptive.'

'Oh,' he said, 'it is your dog isn't it?'

'No mate. That's our dog, mate, if it's anybody's, whether you like it or not. So he's only partly mine. Have you paid your part of the registration? If that animal came to my door and I could feed it I'd do so, I wouldn't ask it to stay and it wouldn't hear me if I did. I don't believe I'd ever have the right to detain him, but he's as free as I am and he has the right to move when and how he chooses. There's only one thing that could stop 'im - people like you. If you want that dog registered, I suggest you register it, mate. You do your bit and I'll do mine. And I can do that with every dog you come to.' But why not do it the easy way and let the dog come to you. And let 'im leave when he's happy to do so, if he doesn't like the tucker. Or he mightn't like the company.

If he likes both, he'll stay, and you've got a real friend. You didn't have to buy it, you didn't have to register it, you didn't have to detain it, you didn't have to do a thing. Only say 'Matey, you've been a great cobber. I've enjoyed your company. Come again someday and next time I hope it's a sausage.'

It's just the same for a cat or a person, as far as I'm concerned. They're all the same, all creatures of God. No-one's better than the other and I wouldn't do less for one than the other.

The only difference would be that for a human being he'd get it cooked, that's all.

Animals are very sadly mistreated. We know very well, if we sit too long in one place, our bowels eventually become bound up. We've got to get a certain amount of exercise to just make our bowels work. When a dog's tied up how can he get that exercise? It's not fair.

What's good for you is also good for the dog.

I can remember when I was younger, any old dog'd happen along. Nobody could order you to tie your dog up - they were all free.

It had good points as well as bad, like everything else in life. The odd person got bit but they still get bit today too. There are a lot of disgruntled dogs around, mate. Because on the odd occasion that they do get off, they take it out on someone, and good luck to them. Pity they don't do it more, but they get shot if they do.

I was livin' under the beach umbrella with the plastic around the outside, and really comfortable too it was, in Grey Lynn in Auckland, in my sister's orchard. And a cat was hangin' around my tent. I couldn't make out why. It seemed to be very skittery runnin' here and there for no reason.

What the bloody hell's goin' on 'round here, I wondered. The next thing I came home at lunchtime and went in to have a snore for a while and as I lay down I heard 'wee wee mee mee' and a blinkin' cat shot out from underneath.

That cat had just had its kittens and they were just like mice. So I pushed them over, a litter of four, to have my sleep. They must've been born under my groundsheet.

Anyway the cat would sit outside six foot away from the door entrance and wouldn't come in. So because I knew she wanted to feed them and lick them, I got out. I stayed out for about three or four hours.

She got used to things from that point on, and she knew when I'd go out, she'd come in, lick them over, look after them and feed them and she knew roughly when I'd be back. If she was wrong, she'd take off as soon as she saw me. But we had an unwritten agreement that she'd have a chance to feed her kittens.

One of those kittens became my first cat, Snowy. He was snow white. There was a jet black one, a grey, and a ginger.

Before he even had his eyes open, he crept right up on my chest. I didn't even know he was there. I felt something scratching and there he was. He just sat there with his little blind eyes just lookin' straight at me. I thought, by crikey, I think this little blighter *likes* me. And I was a bit worried because I didn't know what I was goin' to do with them, Snowy included. But he attached himself to me and wasn't going to be outdone.

With all that, when he finally talked me into taking him with me he thought he was blinkin' Lord Muck. The cat with me now sometimes relents and accepts that we're equal. But not Snowy. Always the kingpin.

But they taught me one thing. They are very thankful when a meal comes their way. And I thought, by crikey, if only I can be as sincere as that in thanking my provider.

People still come up to me sayin' 'Hi!' Remember me? It was ten years ago we last met.' But I can't blinkin' remember everyone ten years ago. Sometimes I meet about a hundred people a day. All and sundry seem to come sometimes. But I think they used to come to see Snowy. He was such a beautiful looking cat, you see.

I wanted to give 'im away but there were no takers. 'Cause he never was particularly happy about *bikes*. One thing though - he knew the bike took him to greener hunting pastures. It was the *going* there he didn't like. But as soon as I stirred in the morning, and he ate, up he'd jump on the seat.

And then I had a hen as well, for a short period. I think it must have fallen off a farm vehicle because it just wandered into my camp one day. It was partly injured but I brought it 'round. I had a hell of a job with it on the bike, although Snowy and him got on alright.

But anything like that, it doesn't matter what it is, you get attached to. It's a hard knock when you lose a little cobber like a pet. I've had Snowy I, Snowy II, and Snowy III. As a matter of fact, Snowy II and Snowy III were not really white cats, they were partly grey, but they did have white on them. So I thought, well, the simplest thing is that seeing I was used to calling them Snowy, I'll call 'em I, II and III. They all came in succession.

Then the next one was a ginger and he was a great little fella. They all had their own character and were just that little bit different.

It's nice to have someone or something to come home to, to welcome you. They want their tea and expect their attention. But when they move they have to move with you. A cat's not like a dog who'll run alongside the bike.

Actually if you had a good dog you could train him to find a bottle for you. And pick it up too. I considered it at one stage, then thought bugger it, it's only another hassle.

A cat has a kind of a time clock in him, and it's pretty reliable. It suddenly clicks in him when it's dinner time. He expects it on the dot. He'll go into quite a hassle if he doesn't get it on time. He'll start doing nasty things to annoy you.

I had quite a lot of fun with the first Snowy because we worked out quite a good system between us. You couldn't take him into the middle of a city just because you wanted to go there. Where I camped had to be near where he could go free and hunt and that, a bit of bush that had rats to chase, trees to climb.

At Okahu Bay I'd put him on the bank across the road after breakfast and away he'd go. When I came home at night I'd get him some fish. And what fish there! Regular as clockwork I'd catch 'em, big snapper. Never miss. Blinkin' kahawai, everything. We were in paradise.

I did up a house for someone for buckshee. I did it because I liked her. She was leaving and she had this cat, the one with me now. She didn't know what to do with it. So I said 'Oh well, you know where I live. If there happens to be a strange cat around there I'll feed him.'

So he comes over.

Again someone said to me 'Is that your cat?' And I said 'No, it is not my cat. It's yours and mine. Our cat. That's his name, by the way, 'Our Cat'. And if he has a choice, which is not often, if he has anything it mightn't be very often, but if he does have a choice he likes the best steak for breakfast. Remember,' I says 'you know what his *name* is, you know where he *lives*. If you ever want to pat him he's glad to accept.'

But they all put their foot in it. When they say your cat, if I'd have once said yes, they'd have all been flat out trying to get him out of here. But I put them in a position where they couldn't. And I told them further. Our Cat likes his tucker. So he gets free milk every day, sometimes even biscuits.

Certain ones coughed up, certain ones didn't. Some come through with a fish.

I can always tell people he likes. There's three different kinds of people to him. There's some he likes, some he's not so sure of and some he can grow to like with a little persuasion of the right kind, which means fish.

He's got fish on the bloody brain, that bugger!

This fella says 'I've got a lot of bones here. They'll be alright for the cat.'

I said 'No they won't. Not for Our Cat. Our Cat eats the best of fish. He eats wholesome foods, or if he can't get it from your fridge mate, he can do it from the sea and that takes time. He has a fair go. What his cobber gets, oh well, that's not so important. But nobody insults Our Cat by giving 'im bones. Especially bones with nothing on it. From here on down I'll be fishing for three days. Our Cat's gotta be *fed*.'

No, Our Cat likes the real thing. He's not interested in fish bones thrown to him as leftovers. Offer him bones *and* fish and you may get him interested. You can do that to me and maybe I'll settle for bones.

This cat counts potatoes too. He knows when I have one more than him. He gives me this filthy look when that happens.

Sometimes he'll tell you he's hungry, then when you chuck something down, he won't eat it. There's more reasons than one why. Sometimes he's got a mate waitin' out there. As soon as it's dark and he sees my light go out, he gets his mate to come in. And gives it to him.

Sometimes he does it quite different. He says 'I couldn't care less what *you* think. you're only second around here. He brings his mate in here in broad daylight. And he says 'Now if you're gonna feed me, *feed* me.' So I feed 'im, he backs off, and gives it to the other one. In front of me eyes.

This cat, he loves watching cars. The very thing that I hate.

You might see him rubbing his head. That's a sign of rain. You can always tell how much rain, too. When he holes up at the foot of my bed, that's three days rain. No mistaking it. But when he just sits in the doorway there, aw maybe a day, not much of that either. But a lot of rain and he won't move from the foot of my bed, he just takes my bed over until the weather stops.

He's got complete control here. If he wants to sleep on the table he sleeps on the table. No questions asked. On another night he says it's too easy, I'll try a different way. He sleeps here, there, this way 'round, then the opposite, all 'round the clock. Just to let me know that he's boss.

After he found I couldn't care less he ended up on the mat. What he wanted me to do was shoo him off everywhere, just to get my attention. But it never worked. I didn't, so he gave up in the end.

He and I get along really well most days, rarely argue; we do have a bit of a tiff now and again, but not much. We're only joking anyway, even then.

What do we argue about?

Well he's got the same as I've got, believe it or not, when it comes to the world. Likes his little joke. Let's you know it too, pretty quick. He doesn't think he's any worse than me, and I have to agree. We're all God's creation.

I don't see why a man should think himself so blinkin' important, and more than anything else. They're flesh and blood too. Do you know, he actually kisses the fish before he eats him. He says I love you so much that I'm going to eat you. That's a fact. He rubs himself on it and purrs. Well when you look at it you can only say that it's a pure love, that's all. He doesn't even see that the fish is dead.

The first Snowy used to charge bulls. He'd put his little head down and ram them if they got too close to us and our camp. Yeah, just like a goat. Well this cat with me now has a similar trick. He rams *me*! While I'm asleep too!

Generally I talk out aloud to meself while I'm thinking. It puts thinking into reality. Otherwise thinking can be a form of hiding.

Once I went to sleep talkin' to myself aloud and suddenly the cat landed on me. I woke up with a start and found that I was still talkin', and the same sentence as when I went to sleep!

The cat said 'I can't sleep with all that racket. And besides, it's boring me.' Sometimes he says 'I'm goin' outside to sleep, to get some *peace*.'

And sometimes too when he wants an extra drink of milk at night he jumps on my chest. Boom! I'm sound asleep and he wakes me with a hell of a start. And if I don't get up smartly he knocks things off here and there and makes a hell of a bloody racket. Makes out he's playin' mice, you know, but all he's doing is wakin' me up.

He wants his blinkin' grub and quick.

Lately, however, I must say, he's gotten out of that habit and he's decided to take his meals with me. Nobody taught him that but his god. Now not even humans have got his manners.

He comes in and sniffs to see if my tucker's on the table before he goes near his own, just to make sure I've got a feed. The odd bird he catches, he brings in.

Old Snowy used to do that too, he used to lay a bird at my feet. He'd say Look, you've been feeding me long enough mate. Only once in a while do I get a chance at feeding you so here you are.

Now I've eaten mynas and they're good eating too. They were game birds once. There are a lot of things you wouldn't dream of eating but they're quite wholesome. In some countries people eat starlings and they're only half the size of a myna.

Once I caught no fish, not a sprat, and I looked at my cat and he looked at me.

There was this understanding.

I said 'Sorry mate, I can't feed you tonight.' I wasn't too worried about me, I could go days without anything.

Snowy went away and came back with three blackbirds.

Dead.

He laid 'em at my feet.

So I made a pie. You've heard the nursery rhyme, baked in a pie. I thought I'd try that.

I'd have to say it was nicer than chicken.

Now and again my cat just won't settle for anything. He shakes his head and says No, I'm a bit sick o'that all the time. He tells you by goin' from one thing to another.

He picks up one thing, nah, no dice, put down something else, no dice, gives a sniff at it, and then on. He might have a nibble at it, then a think about it. If he has a second nibble then you know you've hit the jackpot.

He likes a bit of pumpkin, and the middle of a cabbage. Man, that's sweet.

I happen to like that too.

So we argue about who's gonna have it!

I says 'It's no good for cats but you can have a little bit, just to keep the peace.'

Cats like everybody to know it. Even a king can't laugh at one, mine's always saying. He might smile at him, but not laugh. 'When I'm in my house,' he says, 'I do what I think fit. You can do the other thing, whatever that is.'

This one, he likes to lick my beard, likes to keep it nice and soft and clean. Really cares for me, I don't mind a bit.

The other Snowy used to do it too.

He has my well-being at heart. If you want to see God, there he is, in that cat. You don't have to look far, do you! I can see right into his heart, and he can see right into mine.

The only difference between him and me is that he eats too much fish.

SuperTramp

Ken Ring

Verbal Encounters

"This guy come up to me and says 'Don't you ever work?' I said 'Yeah. I work alright. I'm workin' overtime right now havin' to talk to you."

They used to come up to me with all kinds of questions. Like fella once said 'What do you do if it rains?'

I said 'Look, what do you do?'

'Oh, I got me car.'

I said 'What if you didn't have a car? What if you was me, what'd you do?'

'Aw,' he said, 'I don't know.'

'Well,' I said, 'you'll have to do some homework pretty quick; it's gonna rain matey! Have a look!

Now watch me and see what I do.'

You're continually in the public eye. You have to observe a strict code of conduct. And because I kept bein' asked the same old questions again and again I decided I would always answer in truth if I could, and give a completely different answer each time, so I was answering the same question in a thousand different ways. That way I thought the questions would be more useful to me and whoever happened to be doin' the askin'.

People have said to me 'Don't you get afraid, bein' out here all by yourself?'

I'd say 'Afraid? Where would be the point in bein' afraid? Crikey dick, I could walk out in the bloody road there and somebody might stick a knife in my back. That's more likely than somethin' happenin' to me here. No, there's plenty more things to be afraid of than just livin' in this way.'

A man came up once and asked 'Where'ya goin'?' And I was on my way toward Cambridge, from Auckland.

'Aw, to Auckland,' I said.

'Well you're goin' the wrong way mate,' he said, rubbin' his head and looking at me in amusement.

'No, look at it this way,' I said. 'We live on an island, don't we? Eventually, wherever I go, I have to turn around somewhere; it might be at Wellington or it might be somewhere else; and make my way back. Sooner or later I'll return to where I started from.

And I suppose I'll be doin' some campin' and fishin' on the way.'

I was on a picnic spot, chatting to a camper. One or two other campers were dotted around. It was the beginning of the holiday season. A car drove up towing a huge caravan. The driver got out of his car and came along. He must've assumed I was a blinkin' caretaker.

'Can you camp here?' he asked.

'Why're you askin' me?' I said. 'I'm here, same as you. Please yourself.'

'Is there power anywhere?' he said.

I pointed to the pylons in the fields in the distance.

'Over there. In them wires,' I said.

Then he looked around this mostly empty field that we were all in and his eye caught sight of a small wooden frame around some trees that the council had put up. A sign on it said Keep Out Trees.

He pointed to it and said 'That says keep out. What's the story?'

I said 'If you can get your caravan in there, do it, but there's easier places to park.'

Some are like babies. They want to be told where to go. They're funny the way they see things.

A fella came to me one day and he said 'Aren't you cold?'

I said 'Cold? What d'you mean, cold?'

'Oh,' he said, 'in short pants.'

I said 'Have you got any kids?'

He said 'Yeah.'

I said 'Do they go to school?'

'Yeah.'

'Are they in short pants? 'Cos you'd better do somethin' about keepin' your kids warm. And what about that sheila gettin' across the road down there? In silk stockings or none at all. She must be a helluva lot colder than me. Why don't you go along and ask her? Why me? I'm as warm as blinkin' toast!

If anybody should be warm it'd be me, because of the amount of activity I do. The blood is circulatin' fast. It keeps you warm. The only time I ever get cold is when I've got nothin' to do, loungin' around, even on a hot day.

I find I can go all year 'round in perfect comfort wearing jandals. I never get cold in the feet. Just to go cycling warms my feet, because they do all the work.

People don't know themselves. Or how to use themselves to the best advantage. They don't know how to be warm, nice and beautifully warm and WET and happy. And they don't know how to be nice and comfortably cold.

A lot of people are freezin' stiff, and you're dancin' about in the morning in your bare feet. Straight out of bed and onto that grass in bare feet and brewing up.

I do that regularly.

A lot of people wouldn't give kak for anything I'd say. They just think you're a blinkin' lunatic. And they tell you so, quite often.

Somebody once said to me 'There's a fella been lookin' for you, his name is Dave.'

I said 'I don't know him.'

'Oh, she says, 'you know 'im alright.'

I said 'I don't. I know who I know.'

She said 'Well, he knows you.'

'Well well,' I says, 'he's like a lot of blokes that I'm supposed to know. I don't know them at all. So he doesn't know me.'

Then another fella came to me when I was fishin' out there and I'm buggered if he didn't say the same. He said 'I was reading some cycle magazine or something and a fellow by the name of Dave was lookin' for you.'

I says 'Oh God Almighty, that guy again. That's the guy that used to travel all 'round with me when I was cycling, is that him?'

He said 'Yeah.'

I said 'Well you tell him from me if ever you see him that I've never seen him in my blinkin' life!'

It's funny how you meet people like that. And it comes back on you years after, if ever you ever saw him.

(I would watch Bruce on a winter's morning, running around in bare feet and shorts, a parka on and a beret, getting water in a shallow dish to have his daily wash, come wet or fine weather.

He used cold fresh water, without removing his clothes. He would wash his feet then his head and would then remove just one side of the parka. He would wash there, replace the arm and, then remove the other arm and wash that. I knew he didn't wear underpants, because I never saw him wash any. Yet he was

SuperTramp

scrupulously clean.

His little camp was always neat and tidy when you looked in, as if he was always expecting a visitor. Clothes were folded nicely as was his bedroll. Very army-like. To wash his clothes he always used seawater and sodium carbonate, washing soda crystals, which he said made the clothes soft and preserved them. Then he would hang his wet clothes quite a distance from his camp. I think this was so his little tent didn't attract attention.

When you stood next to Bruce he smelled rather like a sweet fire; he had no body odour or sweaty smell. All his clothes were smoky as you would expect, but there was a leathery smell too and there was something honest and healthy about it.

Bruce's hands were a little unusual for a tradesman, and especially an old carpenter: they were quite fine, with fire-black under the nails. Not what you would call a carpenter's hands. Although not powerful, and part of a slight physique, they were quick and sure hands and the strength was there if needed.

Actually Bruce did know this Dave but under another name, that of Kim Davy. But he only ever called him Kim. I received this story from someone else long afterwards.

Kim had a gypsy wagon that he towed with a tractor. He would get local work as a chef at some of the hotels and tourist resort restaurants and then move on.

On one occasion when we were all together at Waiotahi, Bruce and Kim had a spat and fell out of favour. Apparently Bruce invited Kim over for a meal and Kim was disparaging. Something about Bruce's idea of a pressure-cooker. Of course, Bruce didn't possess one and he decided he urgently needed one to cook this meal. Rather than borrow Kim's, Bruce made his own - an ordinary saucepan with the lid on upside down and heavy rocks placed on top. Worked very well according to Bruce. You could vary the rocks to adjust the pressure!

But they argued over its merits. It developed into a big fuss. According to Bruce, Kim said 'You can't talk to me like that, I'm on a higher plane than you.' And Bruce had replied 'Well, don't forget it, mate, I'm a Boeing, when it comes to higher planes, and nothing flies higher than a Boeing.' Kim moved off shortly after and I don't think they ever saw or spoke to one another again. I also never saw Kim again.

But at the time, Kim had his own little fund of Bruce-tales. Kim's favourite was when Bruce was sitting on the pavement once with a fishing line down an open man-hole. Someone came along and asked him what he was doing. 'Fishing', said Bruce. 'Well you won't catch anything there!' 'You're *wrong', Bruce had apparently said. 'I've just caught you haven't I?'*

A fella some twelve years ago owned a house near where I did a bit of fishing.

'Oh,' he said, 'Gidday, mate.'

I said 'Gidday. Who are you?'

'Oh,' he said, 'don't you know me?'

'I don't know you from a bloody bar of soap matey.'

'Oh,' he said, 'I was talkin' to you.'

I said 'So! So? So was ten million more at different times. Identify yourself. Who are ya?'

He said 'I'm Gary, don't you know?'

I said 'Gary? Never heard the name in my bloody life before.'

'Oh,' he said, 'don't you remember that day, it was rainin' like hell. I was talkin' to you wonderin' if you was gettin' wet.'

I said 'It didn't mean much to me. How long ago was this?'

'Oh,' he says, about eight or nine years ago.'

I said 'How long was I talkin' to you?'

He said 'Oh easily twenty minutes.'

I was supposed to remember twenty minutes I was supposed to have had talkin' with 'Gary' out of thousands of people that I've met in eight or nine years. But because I didn't recognise him, oh gee, you couldn't possibly forget who I am.

Me, Gary, you know me!'

That's the type of thing you come across anywhere, it doesn't matter where you are. Sometimes you wonder if it's really worth bein' on the road for all the hassles afterward; they swear blue blind they know you well. When you think of human beings I'm afraid you can only do one thing and that's laugh. You can only put it down to something that was meant to work and run smoothly, but something went amiss somewhere. That's how I see the world. Of course your own attitude can make all the difference. If you're serious minded, anything a person says to you is taken seriously. Some people are not joking at all, but when they're Gary and you met them for twenty minutes, you should remember them forever.

Then the next thing you know, he's over here again.

'You'd better come over to my place and talk about old times,' he said.

I said 'Yeah, all about that twenty minutes. Must've been a hell of a lot happen in that twenty minutes, mate.'

'Oh,' he says, 'come over anyway.'

People'd say to me, havin' a joke at my expense, 'You've got everything you could have on that bike, what are you going to do with all that stuff?'

I'd say I use this for this and this for that for a start, until I got used to their questions, and I began to learn a little bit. Some of the questions were drivin' me mad because they were always the same. And I grew tired of giving the same answers so I started varying them, tryin' to answer differently each time.

One thing they used to say to me often was 'Okay, you've got all that but you haven't got the kitchen sink.'

I'd say 'Don't be bloody mad. Look, tell you what, put your wallet down there mate, and you bet me that I can't produce a hundred kitchen sinks. And I'll tell you somethin' else. I'll throw in another hundred. Now, put your money down.' Not a one ever took me up.

And it wasn't bluff. I used a piece of black polythene. Now

how did I get two hundred kitchen sinks from a bit of plastic? Quite easy, all I had to do was to move it from one place to another. Each time I used it, it was different!

One way was to just go into a place where there was long grass and stomp around in a circle for a minute. Then I'd put the plastic down where I'd been stomping. Finally I'd stomp right in the middle of it and make a hollow. I'd take my half gallon jug of water from the bike, tip it in, and the grass around the edge would hold the sides of the plastic up like a basin.

I could wash me dishes in that or I could have a bath in it, but I used to say 'sorry sir, ah, at the moment I'm not in the kitchen I'm in the bathroom, ah would you like me to introduce you to the kitchen, to number one of the hundred?' All I had to do then was to hop out of the bath and pull the sheet.

The plumbing never missed.

It never blocked, ever.

And then I turned the sheet up the other way and that was the sink. How could I tell the kitchen from the bathroom? The kitchen side had a piece of sticking plaster to mark it! The mark made sure I always did my dishes in the sink and never in my bath.

So there was the bath and there was the sink-bench all together in one, as many as I wanted, all in my hip pocket.

If I wanted I could take the spare tyre off my bike; in fact I always carried two. I used to stick them one on top of the other and put the plastic down in the middle of that.

When I filled it up with the half gallon of water I could have a wash anywhere, right there and then, on a concrete path even, in the middle of a city.

The same piece of plastic was also my windbreak. You could dig a hole in the sand any size you liked, put the plastic in as a sink or bath, and then the water. You could have double kitchen sinks or triple, side by side if you desired. 'So I haven't got the kitchen sink, mate?'

Wrong! How many would you like?'

Then they'd say 'Oh but you can't have a hot bath.' They were wrong again. I could have it hot, cold or medium. I could soup it up thermostatically, turn it on, turn it off, and get a similar result to a regular bath with taps.

How?

The way I did it once was when I was up at Hicks Bay. I hollowed out some soft papa mud rock and made a hole six feet long and about a foot deep. I hollowed it just beside the river. On the very bottom of the pit I put dry grass, so the bottom of me backside wouldn't get too uncomfortable. You don't get such consideration in a house bath!

Then I put my black plastic lining in, on the bottom, comin' up the sides and lippin' over 'round the edge. Finally a bit of white plastic just on the bottom, laying on the black.

The river was beside me. I just had to bale it into the bath. It was good fishin' at that spot too. I could clean up before dinner while I caught dinner.

At times I didn't even have to dip water from river to bath because the top of the hollow was just about level with high water mark. It used to lap over nicely.

I'd leave it for about an hour. When the sun had heated it, I folded more black plastic over the top to act as a cover. This little manoeuvre really turned up the heat. Why?

The little light that got through the black plastic hit the white bit at the bottom and bounced back again. So you had a kind of thermal action plus the black colour which absorbs heat. It all added to making it get hotter quicker. And all the heat was kept in by the plastic on top.

You didn't have to pin the cover down. It stuck to the water when you put it on. When you tried to take it off there was quite a suction and you had to slide it off, pulling it from the side like a tablecloth.

Well, it got so hot you couldn't get in it. So you adjusted it by dipping cold water in from the river beside you, sittin' in the bath as you worked it. Not much different from what you do in a modern bathroom really.

So when people said 'How d'ya get on when you want a nice hot bath? I could say 'Piece of cake mate. I could do a number of things.

What I could do, is listen to the radio. Why?

To find out the weather. If I'm gonna have a bath I need to know at least a day ahead if there's gonna be any rain. Because if there's no water handy I'll need the rain to fill up my hole!

Then I'd have to cover it up and wait for it to become sunny again so I'd get hot water!

That'd be one way of gettin' water but I never had to do that because water's everywhere in this country. You just need a container to carry it.

But if I had to wait for rain, I could have. Waiting didn't mean a thing to me. I could fish meanwhile, read, I could rest, enjoy the radio. Crikey. A day or two meant nothing.

Sometimes I'd say 'I can wash without a bath, without a river, or the sea.'

'But how?'

'Well,' I explained, 'you can get your feet pretty clean by just goin' for a walk in long wet grass. It gets in your toes and wraps itself around your feet and drags the dirt off. It's quite abrasive.

I used to wash clothes like this too. I would rub soap on and drag them through the grass behind me. The grass acts as a brush. I learnt that, oh, years ago, from me Mum. That's how she washed carpets when she worked in the hotels. My mother taught me a lot of things, although most of what she taught me was bloody rubbish.

You can clean dirty greasy dishes and pots with nothing more than handfuls of grass too. And if it's raining, I take my wet clothes off and hang 'em in the rain. After all, I have plenty of supplies - three sets of clothes; two sets of day clothes.

Water can be collected from the grass too, by wearin' socks or long pants or rags tied to your ankles, goin' for a walk, then wringin' them out every now and then into a container. It's an old army trick. Stick 'em on again, walk some more in the grass and get another lot.

This is where a man operates in need. You don't need a bath every day out there because it's just not as convenient as in a house to go and turn it on whenever you want it. So right away it's regulated how many baths you have. The environment and weather have a bearing on it. It could be a month since you had the last one.

You could have a really good soak, and with almost nothing, even get dressed for the ball after it! I could tell you how *that's* done.

You'd put a sack over your head, cut a hole in the top for the neck, two holes in the sides for your arms and away you'd go. The guy'd look at you and say 'Oh, we only accept the ones that're properly dressed. You're improperly dressed sir.'

You'd say 'Hardly matey! This is a fancy-dress ball isn't it? I'm Robinson Crusoe!'

If you put yourself out on the road with no visible intention of tryin' to impress anyone whatsoever, you're just tryin' to get a meal, just you and a most ordinary pussy, and yet somehow or other, people are takin' notice of you it appears, and all kinds of people come along and want to talk with you.

They've got a real need, they come with an inquiring mind, and some of them with stupid simple bloody dilemmas. Some with real problems too.

So the very fact that they happen to be there should tell you that you're not alone, that there must be others like them that must be just as interested in me as they are.

In fact, if you take it a bit further, even the bloody seagulls're interested in me.

Anyone who comes to me, I try to give them a rich experience. In my heart I feel that God has versed me for it, and them. But there's no need to appear unnecessarily unkind.

'But where do you get your money?'

'Oh,' I says, 'there's two forms of money, coin and note. One type rolls and the other blows. And they both get to me those ways at times.'

One guy says to me 'Aw, you're in the habit of shootin' your mouth off.'

I said 'You never said anythin' truer. Get yourself a lot to shout about mate.'

We're not kids anymore and we're not in the kindergarten. Sometimes if we want to make ourselves felt we have to hurt people. Many are so dumb today, so stereotyped.

This business of everyone helpin' one another is rubbish. People are busybodies. They get in each other's road. They stop people helpin' themselves.

I was condescending like that once too. I didn't like to hurt people's feelings. Now I see that you have to be cruel to be kind. You have to sacrifice yourself and your condescending manner.

You've got to be true. You've got to be blunt. Few words.

Put your message across in a way they'll never forget. You can get hurt too, because they can turn out to be smarter than you. They're just like children sometimes, goin' 'round askin' others to do all their work for them, which takes all their pleasure away.

A lot of them are also lacking in yet another important attribute: the patience to stop and hear you out when you answer their question. So you keep on as long as you can and when they look at the clock and say 'Oh, I gotta go now,' they've made up their minds that they're smarter than you are. Yet they're askin' you to answer their bloody questions and solve their problems in life.

And they have all sorts of funny hassles. One fella came to me a couple of times when I was out there fishin', and the first time he seemed to be agitated, jumpy and that. 'I saw you fishin'' he said, 'fishing here often. You seem to spend a hell of a lot of time here. Isn't it a waste of time?'

I said 'If I thought it was matey I wouldn't be here.'

He said 'Well, what can you see in it?'

I said 'What I can see is what I don't see. Eh?'

He said 'What?'

I said 'Yeah! And I mean that!'

'Oh,' he said, 'well, what don't you see?'

I said 'That's what I see!'

He must've gone home and slept on it because he arrived back one day, all the way from Whakatane just to see me and tell me that he'd decided I'd been speakin' in *parables*.

He said 'I want to know a bit more about that. I'm thinking you've been making a bloody fool out of me.'

I said 'Aw,' don't be silly mate. There's no more soft hearted person. I've got a heart o'gold! I wouldn't hurt you for worlds, mate.'

He said but you said this and you said that.

I said 'Is there any law against it? You came here and asked me the question. Well, you got the answer. If I'd've said nothin' to you, I'd've still been wrong, wouldn't I! I just answered in the best way I considered would help you, that's all.'

When he got up and went, I found two dollars in my box.

He'd left it.

Funny eh?

So all the time you could be workin' without knowin' it.

What I had said to him was: doesn't it remind you of the Almighty? It was a beautiful day. And I said to him that's what I see, yet I don't see it.

That to him was speakin' in parables. I had to contend with that and fish comin' in all at once. There were three or four people standing there as well, firin' questions at me while I was tryin' to land the fish, so I had to talk to them all at the same time. Crikey, talk about hassle - and people suggest that I don't work!

But what are you really out here for?' this jumpy fella kept askin.'

'I'm out here to be with God,' I said. 'You find him easier out here than in town and he can find *you* more easily. You can concentrate better in the peace and quiet and he can see you more easily with no buildings in the way.'

'Oh, if I did it, everybody'd say this, and say that.'

I said 'They might say it to me, too. And they get the same answer all the time. I come here to be at peace, knowin' that things're gonna hot up before long. So don't think that I've got it all in the sense of peace - I have got it all, but all. I've got a thousand things to do at one time. And yet you could look at me and think that I was doin' nothin'.'

Sometimes I have to resort to Christ and religion to explain something. I gradually angle them 'round, like I do the fish, and get them interested before I get them on that tack. Get 'em hooked and then I open out. Bring in the Big Guns.

One guy says 'Oh, you're a religious man.'

I says 'Am I?'

'Yeah,' he says, 'you know you are.'

I said 'No, I don't know anything of the kind. I'm no more religious than you are. What's your thing? Racehorses? Or is it rugby? You must have one somewhere. Don't put it all on me.'

He said 'You know what I mean.'

I said 'No. You tell me what you mean.'

'Well, you believe in a creator.'

'Yeah of course,' I said, 'damn it all mate, something must've created me.'

Most people's religion today is money and nothing else. Along comes a guy, loaded with dough and wants you to stand talkin' to him all day. It's no trouble to him, he'll eat that night as sure as God made little apples. His bank account's full. But there's nothing sure about it for you. Yet he expects you to stand there and talk to him until he decides to pull out.

I had a reporter in Auckland visit me and Snowy. He wanted an interview.

I said 'Look, you get paid for what you're doin', don't you?'

'Oh,' he said, 'I'll say I do. I'd be a bloody mug not to, wouldn't I?'

I said 'That's not my hassle. All I know is, if you was me you wouldn't. And since you get paid for standin' here talkin' to me, I must get paid for standin' here talkin' to you. Because I'm not doin' anything profitable toward myself. I'm not livin' this way for publicity reasons. Actually I'm too well known already for my comfort. I could be fishin' now. I'm not. So what am I goin' to get?

More importantly, what's my *cat* goin' to get? He's in the picture too, you know, the picture in this case being that photo you just took.

He likes to eat too. You're a professional, you get paid for your work. In a sense, me and Snowy are professionals too. Snowy, if I know anything about it mate, works for jelly-meat. That's what he likes, and plenty of it!

Me, if I have to go without, well I don't mind. But I will mind if my cat has to go without. I will mind if you can stand there and get paid for it and I can't.

So I'm puttin' it on you. Jellymeat mate. My pussy'll earn his business because you'll get his picture.

'Well,' he says, 'how much jellymeat do you want?'

I said 'Look at it this way. When it comes to how many photos you take of my pussy, snap as many as you want. The sky's the limit. Same with jellymeat tins. Sky's the limit matey.'

It came out beautifully. Snowy perched like a jockey on the bike. He got about ten pound of jellymeat too. As a matter of fact the Auckland Star and the Herald were competing against each other for me. But one offered jellymeat and the other offered only cash.

'What do you hope to achieve?' one reporter in Tauranga asked me.

'Do I have to achieve something?' I said. 'When you're doin' something you enjoy, it's not a triumph to have achieved it.'

Then he took down some notes about my lifestyle and he misquoted me. So long as Snowy got fed though, I didn't care too much what they said.

But before I got out of Tauranga people were sayin' 'There he is, there's the guy in the article. The one who said he can walk 'round the island for less than it would cost for a gallon of gas!'

I had gone into this garage to fill up my water flagons because close by was my first camp; it was always in the same place. I'd have plenty of water for a shave and a wash and a cup of tea that night and in the morning before I pulled out.

And these people were pointin' and shoutin'. I'd forgotten about that reporter the day before and it took me a while to figure things out. 'Oh there he is, there's that fella!'

So I said 'Is that so!'

'Oh,' this one said, 'it's in the Bay Times, you said you could walk around etc.'

I said 'I said nothing of the kind. I've done it on a lot less, and that's what I told the reporter. 'Sixpence. That's a lot *less* than a gallon of gas. That was from Auckland to Wellington *only*, too, not all 'round the island. It was the price one way. It would cost me another sixpence to do the other half! Or it could cost me nothing. But I didn't really want it put on paper.'

He said 'It's hard to believe.' So I said 'Put some money up matey. You watch me. You can follow me every inch of the way and you'll find out pretty quick if I'm telling the truth or not.'

He wouldn't have it on. People are out to misinterpret you and cause trouble. Sayin' I could do it for the price of a gallon of gas instead of sixpence!

I could've sued him for defamation.

Another reporter met me on the waterfront road and wanted to know my full name. I was Bruce, and I told him that if they had to mention names that was all they were goin' to get.

Not for any reason that I'm tryin' to hide from anythin' but I have other people to consider, who don't necessarily agree with the life I live. I just don't think it's fair to me to advertise the fact that I'm their brother or sister or son or anything else without their approval.

There's a way out and that's that I'm just Bruce. I don't really know what me name is. But Bruce is what I used to be so it'll suffice. I don't sign cheques anymore. I don't even know if I'm the same guy anymore.

Besides, there was once a fella by name of Paul. He became Saul after he'd been through a transition that he called a conversion. So what's a name? Paul had no second name, he was just Paul of Somewhere.

Like Lord Ballantrae of Ballantrae, the Governor General.

I wasn't impressed with him. He wasn't very impressed with me either. He looked me over once, feet first.

The other one, Lord Cobham, was more after my own heart. He was great.

I was comin' up the waterfront road and this flash limousine with its flag fluttering came past with a convoy of cars behind. I thought it was a funeral. I was ready to take me cap off.

Well he saw me stop, that's Cobham himself, and he leaned right out the window and waved to me. I didn't know what the hell for. I looked around to see who was behind me. It couldn't be me.

But there was nobody else there.

You have to be discerning, and extra-sensitive to different types of people. You can tell and smell 'em a mile off, the ones that've got a grudge or don't like the look of your blinkin' whiskers or something.

I camped at Thornton once, where a lot of caravanners go. I had noticed for some time a little spot right up in the lupins and I had always intended stayin' there for a short camp. So this time, up I went. The very next caravan to come in circled 'round for a while then it came right up and sat bang in front of me. I went out to greet them.

'Look.' I said, 'I thought I was gettin' clear of all you lot. I've been watchin' this area for years and I've never seen a single caravan up here, ever. All of a sudden it becomes desirable real estate as soon as I arrive. I've been very careful to pick the place with the *most* lupin weeds, the *biggest* stones, the most uneven ground. Why don't you go back to where the others are?'

They laughed, and I heard 'silly old fool', stuff like that, a lot of it worse language.

They were youths, about six of them, with some girls too. They set up their caravan then they started takin' over the place, puttin' stuff here and there all 'round me as if I didn't exist.

That night they were drinkin' and shouting 'round a fire and one got a car going and drove it 'round and 'round in a tight circle. Plants and sand and stones and dust shot everywhere and I couldn't do a thing but suffer it. I couldn't sleep above the racket either.

Well I waited 'til it was over and they went to bed. Then I made a fire of my own, up wind of them, and I stacked greenery on to produce smoke. Pretty soon it found its way into every air gap and ventilation hole in their caravan and tarpaulin. They were coughin' and splutterin' and comin' out the sides in their pyjamas to see what was goin' on.

But I was unprepared for what happened next. One burly he-man came over and called me every foul thing under the sun. Before I could get a word in edgewise he did a bit of karate on me. He jumped on my blinkin' foot and punched me in the nose.

Anyway, the next morning they were gone. But I couldn't walk properly for about a fortnight afterwards, and my face swelled up like a balloon.

A man stopped beside me once and began pesterin' me. 'What are ya livin' like this for?' he wanted to know.

'Well what are you livin' like that for?' I said, pointing to his new station wagon.

'You can't ask me that. I'm not unusual,' he said. 'It's you that are strange.'

'Well what's wrong with that?' I said, 'I'm not affecting you am I? I'm not in the way of your new piece of tin going down this road; in fact it seems to me that you're stopping me from carryin' on with *my* business.'

'I've a good mind to run you off the road,' he said, 'you're a disgrace to your age! What're you runnin' from, anyway? You look like you're runnin' from somethin'!

'Me? I'm not runnin' anywhere,' I said. 'But I'll tell you one thing matey, I predict that within the next ten minutes it'll be you that's doin' the running, full speed down this road away from *me*!

That was it. He slammed his new front door and took off at a hell of a rate. He nearly knocked me over in the process.

On occasions they used to stop and offer me rides, before I had the bike. But I scotched that one very early in the peace. Carloads of young fellas'd pull over just ahead, wait for you to be nearly in, then pull out. One lot did that three times. I vowed never again.

I thought my soul was worth more than saving a few hours walk. To get in would be lettin' 'em buy my soul.

So I put it the other way 'round. If I saw a guy stop and if I thought that he was at that racket at all, I used to put it on him. I'd say Gidday and keep going. 'Nice day!'

But one bloke, be begged me, to get in his bloody car. I was going through a gorge near New Plymouth. This big flash car pulled up and he said 'Can I give you a lift?'

I was walkin' and I had my big sack.

I said 'No thanks mate.'

He said 'What?' I see you've got a hell of a load there.'

'Nah! This is nothin'. It's only half full! When you see me

carryin' it across my shoulders, you'll know I've got a *sort of* a load.'

I had to carry it by the ears across my shoulders eventually; it was a coal sack and so big that when it was full that was the only way to carry it. It had all my gear and fifty bottles and all my tucker; everything in there, I never had to go back one step ever.

I said 'I'm not bullshitting.'

He said 'Oh, I can't understand you.'

'Well,' I said, 'why try? I'm not tryin' to understand you mate. I often wonder what makes people like you tick though. Here's a beautiful day, and you're shut away in a box, made of tin at that, and you expect me to do it your way too. That's the part that annoys me!'

He said 'Oh,' and he seemed a bit stuck for words.

I said 'You wouldn't do it intentionally, you're not that kind of person, I don't think. But really, I would've preferred that you hadn't stopped at all mate, not because I didn't want to know you, but because I know what you're gonna ask me, and I'm not on matey. I've learned things that've taught me what to do, when, and how. I don't need to be told to, and I can't see any good for me gettin' in your car.'

'Oh, you'll get there quicker.'

'What for? Where am I going? Eventually, I'll arrive back at this point, having gone around in a circle. I want to make time *spin out!* So where's the point in rushing the situation? You're gonna rush from one town to another, and you're gonna be at a loose end as to what to do when you get there. No, there's so much to be had out here. If you were wise matey, you'd leave your car right where it is, forever!'

He said 'Look, I know you mean what you say, but somehow I just can't believe it, even though I know that what you say is true. I haven't met anyone like that before, who talked like that and really meant it!'

I said 'Well this is really something; you want to stick with it mate, listen, open your ears, but don't move one inch. Park right where you are and listen.'

And I into him then, and told him all a few points about where I thought he was goin' the wrong way.

He said 'Look. I've got plenty of money. I can have everything I want'

I said 'Doesn't mean a thing to me, mate. Money is not the basis of my values. In fact, all it tells me, and I hate to say it, but it shows up a certain weakness in a person. This is the way I see things, and I hope you'll bear with me, you may become a little disgruntled about what I say but to me it's the truth. What I say I mean.

I feel a little sorry for you, because I know there's a big road just ahead of you. You're not goin' to zoom along now, if you leave your car there. You're gonna be draggin' your bloody heels before night's out. But you're gonna sleep sounder than you've ever slept in your bloody life before and you're goin' to get up in the morning footsore and weary, mate. But today if you stick with it, after two years, you're not gonna be sorry you ever did it.

That's how long it'll take for your apprenticeship. I won't be with you to keep you company but I won't be far behind and I won't be far ahead of you either, but I'm not in a hurry, not that kind of a hurry. I know I'll get where I'm goin' anyway, sooner or later, I don't even know where it is, as far as this world is concerned, but I'll get there.

I'm sure that I'll have more time to get there the slower I go. I'll live longer, more healthily and more contented. So I'll have longer to do the journey, won't I. So I'm more sure to get there than you are mate, with all your bloody rush.

Do you hear anything?'

I looked at that moment for a spark in his bloody eye.

He said 'What?'

I said 'Look mate, it's time I got goin' There's a life to be lived out there. I can't live it here. If I thought I could say anything to you that would change you, and it's only a glimmer of hope at this stage, I might stick on a bit longer, but the thing is this: I'm not saying that there's no hope for you matey, if you were to do what I said. I don't think it's likely that you'll do it, but maybe if you found out what I say in some odd moment - maybe when you're in bed, or lounging in your sitting room one day, you might think over what I say and maybe a little seed there'll spring to life.

I'm not telling you to do a thing. I'm not even suggesting that you should do it because I've done it. I'm not even saying that if you did do it that you'd succeed. It just did me a hell of a lot of good matey. And I don't see any reason why it shouldn't do for you. But get it straight: I'm not tryin' to say that you should do the same.'

I said to him, 'Look, the way I see it is this, if you even wish you had what I have, which I don't know, but you're obviously curious about me, this tells me something about you, you're not happy.'

'Aw,' he said, 'I have a bit of trouble with me missus.'

I said 'They all say that. But what else d'ya have? Where'd you put your foot wrong? You've been doin' it fairly consistently to be in the state of mind that you're in. I've been rewarded because of a different course in life that I took which was a very dubious course at that time to me, because there was nothing up ahead except a road, that's all. But having gone along the road, I began to find that there was more along there than there was behind me in the big city.'

He said 'I don't know what to do. Not only is my missus giving me trouble but I've got family troubles all 'round.'

He started bringin' out his family woes and all that and he wiped all that I'd been telling him, in favour of his own personal problems.

I said 'Look matey, why don't you forget all your personal problems, they're worldly things. Why don't you take up something new, taste it at least. So long as you live in the old way, you'll be governed in the old way of thinking, the actions and the old people, and you'll be the same old self you were. Life's not goin' to get any better for you.

And it doesn't matter if you get another car in two months' time. It won't be any more value to you than the one you've got. The basis of the ownership of that car is false. The whole basis of your life is in the same category.

You said that I appeared to have something substantial in a way of life and yet you can't agree that you'd rather be out here than over in there. That's what I can't understand. If you're sure, hop out, forget it, leave it there. Just disappear into the unknown and start off onto a new tack.'

Christ told his disciples to follow him. Some made excuses. Some had to go home to see if the missus was alright.

I see no need to agree with everything that was taught or said then. Twelve disciples meant that many different ways of lookin' at the same teaching. I suppose the reason for picking twelve was so that later followers would at least get a general message with a greater degree of chance. That basic message is the interest of humanity.

The guy in the car said 'Somehow I like what you say but I couldn't see me out there doin' what you're doin'. For instance, where are you gonna sleep tonight?'

'Maybe in the willows, maybe in a super bed. It depends what happens between now and bedding down.

You never know, mate!'

The Law

"When I go on the road in the future I think I'll wear different hats. An Aussie hat one day and a turban with me face blacked the next. That way they won't know who I am."

I was working on a scaffold one day down at Point Chev doing a bit of plastering and next thing a couple of jokers came around and crossed the front lawn. By gee I thought, They've got a bloody cheek. It wasn't my place, I was just working there. They came up to my scaffold.

'Are you Collins?' they said.

I said 'Yes.'

'Come down,' they said.

I replied, 'No. Who the hell are you talking to?'

'Well we're Police.'

I said 'I couldn't care who you are, mate, I'm not coming down, you're not tellin' me what to do.'

They said 'We'll come up.'

I said 'Come up, I'm comin' *down*.'

They said 'We want to talk to you.'

'Oh,' I said, 'Good. Then there's no need to come up at all. And I won't have to come down. Go on. Talk. Get crackin'.

'Oh no,' he said, 'We want to talk to you *at length* .'

I said ' Well, get *crackin'*.

He said 'No, we want to take you over to the station.'

'Station? Me? What the hell for?' I said.

'Oh, just a talk' he said.

I said 'I've got no time to talk to you. I'm already behind with this job. I can't be mucking around talking.'

'Oh well, we're ordering you now,' he said. 'You come down or we'll come up and get you and take you down.'

So I went butchers. 'You know you're being totally unfair,' I said. 'I don't really know what you're talking about, what you're hinting at, anything. Here you are, ordering me about on my own job. To say nothing of the people inside the house, who I'm doing the job for.'

In the end anyway, we wound up at the Point Chevalier Police Station. They got me in there. 'When were you last up at Stan's restaurant?' he said.

And I told him. I used to go up, do some dishes and he'd give me a meal. I even waited on tables sometimes. Just to help out.

'Oh.'

He said to his mate: 'That was when he did it.'

I said 'What? He did what? Who was he and what did he do?'

'Oh,' he said 'he was you and you were seen at the scene of the crime.'

I said 'You're bloody mad. You're off your bloody block mate. I never been *at* the scene of a crime, let alone been *seen* at the scene of a crime! I could do better than that, and if I couldn't I'd bloody well take something else on. What crime? You're joking, surely.'

He said 'Are we? Well by the time we're finished with you, you won't think so. You know what we do with buggers like you? You're just a bloody rat-bag.'

They gave me hell, but I never did learn what they wanted me for. I didn't get clear of them till three o'clock in the bloody morning. They took turns on me. When one got tired then the other guy'd have a go. Oh crikey. In the end they conceded that nothing was going to change.

I said that what I'd said was all that I was going to say, besides, I knew nothing of what the hell they were talking about. And I said 'And that's where it'll be forever, matey, you can stay here and I'll stay with you forever and I'll still say the same.'

Then he said something which made me think that someone had tried to frame me.

'Oh' he said, "we know that you did it. Because we've been *told* that you did it'.

I said 'Well you know something that I don't.'

They swore right to the end that I did and they wanted to charge me.

'Well' I said 'Get on with it. Charge me. Don't beat around the bush. Charge me. But remember one thing, something tells me that if you do you're for it matey, and I'm not fooling. But I believe you should do it if you believe what you say. So now I'm challenging you to charge me.

After a while he says 'Come on, let's go.'

'Where are we going?'

'Over to your place.'

'What the hell for?'

'There's something over there we want to find.'

'What?'

'A blue pullover.'

'Oh yeah,' I said 'Well I can't recollect I've got a blue pullover. So you're wasting your time going over there. Give me my bloody key and let me go..'

'We're all going over' he said.

When we got there they chucked everything around everywhere, turned the bed upside down, they went bloody mad. They never found a thing.

That's the kind of shit I've had to put up with. They've had me boiling inside, really boiling, matey. If I tried to put sense into them they just laughed.

On my first trip to Wellington, when I finally wanted to go again I bought a bike in Petone. It was a racing bike, super-light. I bought it with the wages I got from the railway job at Cloburn.

That was the start of my cycling days as an adult.

But I gave it away not long afterwards, with all the other flash gear. So I walked it many times, got other bikes, wore them out, and walked again. In the end I found I *had* to have a bike, to protect me *from the law*. And I'll come to that story.

Although even *with* the bike I got hassled. I was stopped at some lights one night, waitin' for them to change and a cop comes over and says to me 'Where's your light?'

I said 'Can't you see it here, it's an ordinary light.'

'Why isn't it on?' he says.

'Well now mate,' I says, 'the dynamo doesn't go when you stop, now, does it?'

'Oh,' he says, 'you still need lights if you're out at night.'

'Just wait a minute,' I said, 'hang around, and you'll see 'em plain as day.'

'No,' he said, 'you need something *now* as well.'

'Look,' I said,' I'm not silly. This is an ordinary light and an ordinary dynamo and I haven't tampered with it or altered it in any way whatsoever. As long as I've had it, it's only operated when I've moved, and stopped when I've stopped. Now if there's something wrong or something illegal about that then get onto the guy in the shop that sold it to me - I bought it in good faith. It was supposed to be right for the job. Don't get onto *me* about it!'

I've probably always played it too straight. I'd say I wasn't cold and it was always true. To tell some people who had already made up their mind that you're cold, even though you're not, *that* you're not, means you've got a job ahead of you. They've made up their minds before they asked you and that's that.

When you're on the road overall though, it pays to be honest and say things as you see them. You can be wrong, happily wrong. I've run afoul of the law on more occasions than I've needed, simply because I told the truth too much. But I gained from it in the long run, with experiences I wouldn't have otherwise had.

The law itself is a hassle. They didn't stick to ethics.

One fella says to me 'I never see you on the road now.'

'On no,' I said.' 'I've been off it lately.'

He said 'We miss you. We used to like seein' you go past.'

'Well,' I said, 'you're about the only one in Whakatane!'

So you did have a few friends without knowin' it. But the funny thing is, you never seemed to meet them, on the road. You only met the rat-bags. They'd say 'Oh, why can you do that? Oh if I did that, crikey! I'd be run in!'

I'd say 'What do you think *I've* been? I've been run in matey! That was the price! You wanna do it, you do it, but be ready for the consequences. I've got no qualms about it, you must expect some hassle from living unconventionally.'

A traffic cop came up to me on the waterfront drive in Auckland. I had two fishin' lines across the road. The cars were runnin' over them. He said 'What are you doin'?'

'Fishin'.'

'I don't believe you. Why two lines?'

'Well officer, one's for snapper and one's for trevally.'

He stared hard at me. 'Come on, what's goin' on?' he asked.

I said 'Have a look if you don't believe me. On the left one there'll be two snapper.'

He went over and pulled it up. Actually there were three on it. Then he said with a slight smile 'If there's a couple of trevally on the other line I'll go away and leave you alone.' He pulled it up and sure enough there were two there. Real beauties!

At this particular place I had discovered, snapper and trevally gathered only a few feet apart from each other for some unknown reason. And I was catchin' them both, every day without fail!

I thought every time I could have a serve back at the authorities, I would. I was getting such poor treatment that I decided to stop pulling punches. This is where my tongue got me into trouble.

A reporter interviewed me. He said 'What are you doin' now, just at the moment?'

I said 'Fishin'. I do a lot of fishin' you know, especially at night. I prefer it when I'm in bed.'

'Oh,' he says, 'there?'

'Yeah. Right there mate.'

'Oh. Why do you fish when you're in bed?'

'Well,' I said, 'it keeps me out of jail, see.'

'How does *that* keep you out of jail?'

'Well,' I said, 'of all the things they could have you for, they can't have you for fishing, day or night! There's no such law as a no-fishing law and there's no such thing as a curfew, as you well know. I could just lie in bed and maybe they'd consider that I was an idle and disorderly person or something. But they can't when I'm fishin' matey, I'm workin'. So I tie it to me big toe. That puts me to sleep very nice and comfortably.'

They printed it!

And ooh man, did that get them cops goin'!

So I'd be here on the beach, havin' put me bed down, hopped in, stuck my feet out of the end of the bed and toed the line on. Threw the baited hook in. Sometimes I wasn't even really fishin' because I just put the hook on and the sinker and everything and put the bait, which was a pipi, on, but as soon as the bait was eaten off I didn't know, I just went off to sleep.

A cop would often come along. They knew I was there.

Two or three came one night and one said 'What are you doin' there?' In a very officious manner. So straight away I knew they were ready for war.

I said 'Matey, I don't think it's really important, not to me anyway, what I'm doin'. What is more important to me is that I'm keepin' the law. If you *dare* to suggest that I'm not, on this occasion I'll be very, very upset. And I'm standin' on pretty firm ground, even though it's a beach and made of sand. So I wouldn't say too much. I've been doin' my homework. And if you want to find the answers you just go right ahead and do what I think you'd like to do. You'll get them in court. Do you really want to know what I'm doing? Do you? Well I'll tell you. Then you can all go home to bed. And I can go to bed too. Because, I'm fishing.'

'Fishing?'

'Yeah. Fishing.'

'Where? Where's the line?'

'There. On me big toe. Have a look.' I said 'By the way, while you're lookin' would ya haul it in? There mightn't be any bait on it.'

So he started pullin' it in. I said 'There might even be a big fish on it.'

When he pulled it in of course the pipi was gone. So I said 'Here's some pipis here, put another one on.'

'Oh,' he said to his mates 'did ya hear him? Telling us to put a pipi on his line!'

I said 'Yeah. That's because you asked me for answers. Well you got 'em. I was fishing, mate, and the fish took me bait. Well? It's like pickin' a fella up in a patrol car and taking him into the police station to question him. If you pick him up at his home you should run him back again. It's pure etiquette now. You put my line back. You pulled it in.'

He threw it back!

I've had cops doin' all kinds of funny things. I've even had one fella pickin' up bottles for me in a patrol car.

I was just south of Cambridge on this particular day. On a stretch of road just as you leave town is a takeaway bar. The guy who owned it, I'd never seen him before. I started pickin' up bottles and in the end I gave him four hundred and seventy five in a day and a half. There'd been no bottles picked up around there for donkeys' years. It was a very popular bit of road and they'd collected and collected. It was just after I'd started pickin' 'em up, as a matter of fact, and so he was part of an experiment.

I went in there with about a dozen and asked him if he wanted them, expecting an immediate rebuff. He said 'Alright, put 'em on the counter.' Oh gee, I nearly fell over backwards. Then he said 'You know, you get less for the smaller ones.' Well I didn't know. I thought, now I'm startin' to *learn* about this business!

Just as we're goin' out the door I said, 'Oh, just as an afterthought mate, I've got some more on the bike. Would you be interested?'

He said 'Yeah. Bring in as many as you've got.'

I said 'Are you dinkum? Because you may be sorry you said that.'

He said 'Yes. Quite.'

So for the whole day, all I did was walk along pickin' up bottles, stackin' them up by lamp-posts. Then all I had to do was go back along me tracks with one sack.

Anyway I got nearly to the end of the situation. There were

about four or five loads of bottles left. A fella comes out of a house and he grabbed me by the bloody neck and he shook hell out of me. And he said 'Hey, you keep off my property!'

I said 'You're a bloody lunatic! What d'ya mean, off *your* property? I haven't been *on* your property.'

'Ah,' he said, 'the neighbours rung me and told me they saw you on it.'

'Well,' I said, 'your neighbours are lunatics too then, because I haven't been on your property in my life. You go and ring them up and get them over here, and let 'em say it to my face and let me defend myself. This is our property, this road, and I haven't been off it. So you're mad!'

'Ooh,' he said, 'I'm gonna get the cops.'

'You do that, 'I said, 'and just to show you I've not been on your blinkin' property, I'll wait here. I'll not run. But I haven't got all day. I'll give you a time limit, of one hour, and I can't afford *that* either. I have to work for my living. So get those cops here mate, smartly. I'd like to see them as much as you would. So get on your phone!' He tore into his house and rang up.

Sometime later I was still waitin' there. I decided it was time to move, I couldn't wait forever for this bugger, the cops, or anybody else. I could tell them quite truthfully if I had to, that I'd given them an hour.

Since he didn't want me on his property, the only way I could contact him was to yell from the road. I called out 'Hoi, hoi! Hey, rat-bag!' No reply.

Then I looked up the road and here's a squad car bearing down on me at full speed. I thought, oh well, here goes another few hours. But the car got to me and then just kept going, flat out past me. I yelled Hey, hey! They went about a kilometre before they could put the brakes on to pull up.

I said, 'I'm the guy you're lookin' for.'

The cop said, 'What're you talkin about?'

I said, 'It's me you want to talk to. But I'm lookin' for you too, just by the way.'

'Oh,' he says, *'are* you now?'

It turned out that these guys had had no message at all. The fella in the house'd rung the Hamilton cops. And these ones were goin' on another call. Of course because I said what I did in the way that I did, they thought I was goin' a bit loony or somethin'.

'You'd better come with us,' they said. 'Would you just get in there?' Alright. I got in. They turned the car around and went back towards their station.

When we got there this one guy says, 'Now what's all the trouble? Explain yourself. You were actin' a little odd out there.'

I said, 'I was assaulted, not badly, but enough to upset my dignity, while I was goin' about my lawful business. It's the other guy who should be here, not me. Not only have you got the wrong joker, but you're not even the right *cops*!'

'Oh well,' he says, 'what were you doing?'

'Picking up bottles.'

'Er, what for?'

'Well I've gotta eat.'

'Yeah,' he says, 'but you couldn't just eat from bottles.'

I says, 'Couldn't I? You'd be surprised, matey.'

He says, 'What do you do with 'em?'

I says, 'I sell 'em to the dairies and that, you know. I don't sell 'em in the truest sense, I exchange them for food. And that's not illegal.'

He says, 'Have you got any money?'

I said, 'No, but I've got a bit of *potential*. You wouldn't know what it is and I'm not goin' to tell you, either. But it's there and I can produce it pretty quick if I have to, even though I haven't got a penny on me. You lay it on the line and I'll do just that.'

He said, 'Alright, it's on the line.'

'Okay,' I said, but first I'll need ultra-quick transport to get me to a takeaway bar that I know of. So how quick I can produce this money'll depend on *you*.'

Away we went. We got to the place and we walked in. The cop says to the bar fella, 'Er, would you have a moment? This guy here says that you have some money for him.'

'Yeah, I have.'

'What's it for?'

'Oh,' he says, 'I can't see that that matters. It's quite legitimate.'

'Well,' the cop went on, 'we could be havin' this guy up on a charge of idle and disorderly which means he hasn't got any money. But he said you've got some money for him.'

He said, 'That's dead right. And you'd be the biggest liar unhung if you charged him with I and D. He's the greatest worker I've ever seen, bar none. Don't call him lazy. He's bloody fantastic. He came in here with a few bottles asking would I take them. I said, Yeah, bring in all you've got. Well they've never stopped comin' *yet*. But I have to keep my word. And I've been flooded!'

So the cop says to me, 'Alright, how much've you got comin'?' At that stage it was about four or five dollars. 'Okay,' he said, 'let's take you back to the office.'

I said, 'I'm not goin' back there. I've got work to do mate, and you've wasted all my day, frigging around about nothing. The original guy who assaulted me, you've done nothing about. But I'll tell you what I'm goin' to do. I'll let you out mate. I've still got about five bags of bottles there to be picked up; they've got to come here before I get the money and get out of here. It's gettin' near time for me to camp down as a matter of fact.

He said, 'Camp down?'

I said, 'Yeah, but that's another story, and I'll set your mind on that later. In the meantime we've got to get those bottles. *You've* got to make me up for my lost time so *you're* gonna help me. And I'm only giving you one chance to do it, to balance the ledger. Now this patrol car is just the very thing to get them bottles with.'

He said, 'Aw, come on then. Get in.'

And away we went up the road, to the furthest away lamp-post, that was the fifth one from where we were, and we picked up the first bottles. I had me bag with me, I filled 'er up and away we went again and emptied it. He didn't wake up 'til we'd almost done 'em and there was only two bags left.

He said, 'What in the hell are we running back for, every time we want a load of bottles?'

'Oh,' I said, 'I've only got one bag, mate!'

I became quite friendly with that cop after that. He was a sergeant. He said, 'Look, I'm beginning to see that there's another angle with you. I haven't got it all sorted out yet but we've been a little mistaken perhaps. But ever since the last couple of days our phone's never stopped ringing. There've been complaints coming in from all directions. And I think you're the source of them.' He whispered, 'How long are ya gonna stay round this area?'

'Aw,' I said, 'just about how long it takes me to clean up the bottles. I've just about seen the end of them now. But I'll be working the other side of Cambridge then going towards Tirau. So the complaints'll be coming from a different *direction*. But you'll know what's going on now, so you won't have to worry.'

He said, 'Well that's alright. Tell you what, if you're ever doin' this again, anywhere or anytime, give us a bit of advance notice that you're on your way, will ya?'

So I said, 'Yeah sure, I'd be glad to do that. But I'll do better than that. I'll come and visit you and tell you that I'm around. I'll tell you where I'm going to sleep that night and anything else you want to know, even the direction I'm heading in. All you've got to do is ask if you want more.'

So it worked to my advantage. Whenever I came to that town, it always had to be either a Sunday or just on morning smoko if possible. If not, afternoon smoko or lunch. Of course he offered me a cup of tea the first time, and some biscuits, and I remembered it. I thought that if I timed it right, well, here's a free cup of tea just for goin' in there.

I used to say, 'Hiya Sarge, how's things?'

He'd look up and say, 'Oh, it's you. Where'ya going this time?'

I'd say, 'Oh, up the coast.'

'Where'ya sleepin' tonight?' And I told him under the traffic bridge there, down in the little park just out of town going south. It's not used very much. There's some seats there and I used to put me little kerosene stove on the table and do it in style.

'What are you goin' to do when you get up the coast this time?'

'Oh, a bit of fishing and generally enjoy myself. Besides, put it this way, it's part of my system.'

'Okay,' he says.

The next time I go round there, 'Oh, it's lunchtime,' he said.

'Well,' I said, 'That's alright.'

He said, 'Would you like to have lunch with us?' His house was next door to the Police Station. 'Come with me.'

Well it turned out to be a hot dinner.

So I knew when to be there next time!

But they weren't all like him. One night in Auckland I slept outside the racecourse. In fact they didn't catch me sleepin'. I had gotten out of bed and was already cookin' breakfast, but my bed was still there, rolled down.

A squad car pulls up. 'What're you doin' there?'

'Are you talkin' to me?'

'Yeah. What are you doing there?'

'Oh,' I says, 'cookin' breakfast. What d'you expect me to be doin'?'

'Oh. You been here all night?'

I said, 'Well most of it anyway.'

He said, 'Get your gear together, hurry up, and get in.'

I said, 'Just a minute matey, I'm not finished me breakfast yet.'

'Well hurry up!' he said. I was bloody ages doin' it. In the end he said 'Come on, get in.'

'No matey, I'm not gettin' in there. You might like to put me in there but I'm not of my own free will gettin' in. I'm not a bloody imbecile altogether. If you want to arrest me you'll have to arrest me. But remember, where I go, you'll go, for sure. Keep that well under your hat. Now we'll go around to the other side door and I'll get in.'

He said, 'Oh you're not goin' to take off are you?'

'We'll make sure about this, 'I said, 'give us your hand. You're comin' with me.' We went around to the side door and I got in myself. 'Now,' I said, 'I have let you out of a very tight corner because I've half arrested myself. But you still did the other half and some of it'll be on you eventually to suffer whatever I suffer for arresting me for nothing, having done nothing of matter to anybody. Come on, get crackin'. Get it over with.'

When we got there they locked me up.

After a few hours, 'Come on, out the door, we're goin' to the court.' Up we go, and then I'm in front of the judge.

'How do you plead?'

I said, 'I don't.'

He said, 'What? You've got to plead.'

I said, 'No. I don't have to do anything.' The bloody cops in the court then got hold of me and they shook me.

He said, 'Well? You've got to plead!'

I said, 'No. How can I plead? And what about? I'm not a blinkin' sheep!'

'Oh,' he said, 'alright.' And he went mumble mumble to his mates. He didn't know what to do.

'Alright,' he said, 'remanded to Kingseat Mental Hospital for one week and you'll appear one week from now.' By that stage I didn't even care what he said.

After a week I found myself back there again.

'Well,' he said, 'we've decided that you need treatment very badly. If you sign the forms you can be admitted as a voluntary patient. You'll be out of there in no time.'

I said, 'I'm sorry sir, but I couldn't do that, the reason being that I don't think there's anything wrong with me, and if I sign that paper I'm more or less signing my own warrant to say that I'm mental. So I cannot and shall not sign.'

'Remanded,' he said, banging on his hammer. 'You'll be back here in a week.' Okay, and away we went again. Next week, same thing.

'Well? Have you changed your mind?'

'Why should I? It's still the same. If you want to judge me then go ahead but don't ask me to judge myself and say that I'm a lunatic when I'm nothing of the kind.'

He said, 'Is that all you've got to say?'

'Yeah.'

'Right, back you go,' he said. 'We'll see you here in one week's time.'

This went on for six weeks. Once he said, 'Didn't the doctor speak to you before you came here?'

I said, 'Yes, he did. And there were certain threats made, that if I didn't this time sign the paper, I'd be put away for a long, long time. But I still do not sign.'

When they saw that their efforts weren't working, they thought the best thing to do was to get rid of me quickly.

The people who run the institutions are bigger lunatics than the inmates. Even the judge was a lunatic. After all, it took him six weeks to make up his mind. After six weeks of telling me that I needed treatment and God knows what, and tryin' to get me to sign all sorts of forms so that they could treat me, on the final time that they brought me up to court he had the whole of my charge sheet and police file there in front of him. 'Huh! Huh!' he said. 'I can't see a thing wrong with you.'

And I'd just done six weeks. They still convicted me without a proper trial. The conviction wasn't wiped. If that's not a lunatic system I don't know what is.

I've spent time in jail.

I was sent to three different lunatic asylums. I spent eight months in one of them. What for? I still don't know. They said I was idle and disorderly but I wasn't.

That's good isn't it. In your own country. This is the system I went to fight for. Freedom. Democracy. All this shit. And that's one of the reasons that I am what I am.

I object to paying taxes, to build those bloody places, and then to lock me in them. Nor do I pay any policemen wages, just to throw me into prison.

The police came to me once along a waterfront. 'You can't stay here, move on!'

'Where to?' I said.

'Anywhere. We're staying here 'til you pack up.'

I said, 'You're welcome to join me - I'm staying here *too* mate!' They just grabbed my gear and chucked it in the car.

The next thing, we're talkin' to the duty sergeant at Central at *two in the morning*.

'I could book you on idle and disorderly!' he said.

I said, 'You're welcome to try, but you'd better get a big courtroom.'

'Why?'

'Because the rest of Auckland is idle and disorderly at this particular time too.'

The next day the magistrate asked me what job I had and I told him about the bottles.

He said, 'That's no job.'

I said, 'Try it. And see if there's no work in it.'

He said, 'You don't even have fifty cents that would clear you of a vagrancy charge.

I said, 'Look mate, my job doesn't pay me very much. But I'm happy to do it. I'm cleaning the ditches at the same time, doing a community service. No one else seems willing to do it. I've never seen you out there. I've never seen *any* judges out there. You talk about a job. It's hard work just stayin' alive sometimes. Often I go without a meal, too, for a couple of days.'

Most of the rest of the morning consisted almost entirely of police evidence against me, watchin' my movements and that. Finally the judge says, 'Have you anything to say?'

'I sure have,' I says to him, 'You've been doin' most of the talkin' so far, surely it's my turn.'

'Be careful,' he says, 'or you'll be in contempt of court.'

'Oh yes,' I said, 'that's what you want. You don't want to hear my side of things.'

Then he threatened me again with it and he said, 'You know what you are, you're just a nomad!'

I said, 'You're damn right there mate, I am, and what's more, I wouldn't change it for the world! I fought in the war for the freedom to do this sort of thing, or so I thought. So we were told at the time. You look about as old as me. What did you fight for?'

Well, did he see red.

The next thing, I was in the asylum for eight months during which time I had every vile thing that man can do to man done to me. First the full course of shock treatment and then, worst of all, the drugs. Just to break my spirit. It made not one iota of difference to me, I'm no different today than I was then.

When I got out I didn't pick the bottles up for a while and I still got picked on again; once, by a night patrol. They said, 'What're you doing for a job?'

And I said, 'Well I had a job but you people took it away from me.'

For a long, long time I had managed to fob them off in many ways. I really managed to make 'em look goats. I think they found it so hard that they had to get me in the end because I was making a bloody fool of them. That's why on this occasion they sent the whole Task Force after me. It was to get me out of Auckland.

I was in the Central Domain on this particular night, when the Task Force arrived. And this was a real confrontation. They actually started to break up my gear, snapping stuff over their knees and ripping things. There were about twelve of them, all young fellas, and I really told them what I thought.

'You're worse than thugs and blinkin' larrikins, because the people of this city are actually payin' you to do this. Why aren't you out lookin' for real vandals? You're yellow bellied louts - is this what they teach you at Police Academy? Breakin' up the property of a defenceless old joker, twelve of you against one?'

A young cop came up to me once and was askin' me this and that and I told him that I treat everyone as I find them, as individuals, cop or not. But a cop has the police force behind him that he must answer to and this is what time and again has tried to persecute me for bein' different. He asked me how and I mentioned I and D.

'Well,' he said, 'there's a case isn't there?'

I said, 'Look mate, most days now I'm running along ditches, into blackberry bushes lookin' for bottles. Then I have to wash the smelly things. Then I have to cart them to a shop, then prepare myself a meal with next to nothing in the way of modern conveniences. And I have to set up camp. Sometimes it's pelting with rain and sometimes it's freezing cold. But still I have to get them bottles. Often I won't see one for days, sometimes they're everywhere mate. Now I ask you, is that idle and disorderly?'

He cast his eyes away. He looked at his shoes. He murmured, 'Well, it's not idle, anyway.'

SuperTramp

When you know you're workin' your guts out and they tell you you're idle and disorderly, they're making a judgement. But judgement is not for man. He's too gullible. A sinner sitting in judgement on another sinner. Perhaps they mistook me for a wino. Well they didn't get their facts straight.

And where in a big city is a place that people such as me can go for the night? There's the Salvation Army, but who wants that? I carry my own burden, I don't want a hand-out. And who says you have to be shepherded along with them? There's no privacy there, to make you bed as you want it.

They won't let you sleep in the open, in their yard.

The legislators make it hard for people to live in houses. They mortgage them, they keep raisin' the rates, the power bills, the taxes and the general cost of living. So someone opts out and doesn't have these worries. Someone says, 'Okay, I get the message. You must be makin' things hard because you want me to give them up. So here, you have my mortgage and bills and house, I'll go out and wander round for a bit' - but still they're not happy. They make this type of freedom into some sort of a crime.

One day I thought, well, they've had me up so many times on idle and disorderly and I still don't know what it's about so I'm gonna find out.

At the time I had been in Wellington for about two weeks and every night the patrols came around and they seemed to be trackin' me to see where I was goin' to sleep at night. They were worryin' and worryin' me, to the point where I was gettin' pretty ropeable.

They woke me once too often one night. It was the third time in one night, so I just got my gear together, they buggered off, and I headed straight for the Central Police Station.

A big place.

When I got to the counter, I said to the young constable behind it, 'Hey, what do you mean by blinkin' well pestering me the way you do?'

He said, 'What are ya talkin' about? I haven't seen you before.'

I said, 'I'm not talkin' about you personally, it's the whole police in general.'

'Oh,' he said, *'Are you just!'* Then he started gettin' obviously upset. So much so that the sergeants' offices way down the end of a long passage picked it up and heard it. The sergeant came bouncing out.

'What the bloody hell's goin' on here! What's this bloody racket?'

The young constable replied 'Sir, this guy here, he's defaming the Queen's Police Force.' You don't hear folks talkin' like that these days, especially young ones.

The sergeant said, 'What? Are we all crazy around here or something? You get the hell out of it. I'll handle this.

He chased him out, and he calmed down then, and said, 'Well, what's the trouble, mate?'

I said, 'Look, I've only been in this place a short while and

I've been pestered day and bloody night by you guys, when I'm tryin' to go to sleep.'

He said, 'Where are you sleepin'?'

I said, 'In the bus-stop. But I'm discreet. Not until after the last bus is gone. I make that a strict rule.'

'Well,' he says, lowering his voice, 'You can't be sleepin' in the bus-stops.'

I said, 'I know I can't but I know I've gotta sleep somewhere, and it looks like rain tonight, but that's not why I'm really here. I've been pestered by you guys all around this bloody country. It doesn't make sense to me. I'm not hurting anybody. But I've been up several times, I'll tell you straight, on I and D. Idle and disorderly, no fixed abode. I want to know what the law is, what you have to be doing to be doing that, and what it's really about.'

'Hmm, is that so,' he said. 'It's very hard to explain, the law about that one, it's a very comprehensive law. There're many sections of it and it's take me 'til doomsday to tell ya them all. But you look at it this way and you'll never go far wrong.'

No cop did for me what that cop did in a couple of minutes. No cop gave me a cleaner or more effective insight to the law than you couldn've learned at a whole apprenticeship at the college. I got it all in a few words.

He said, 'It's a very comprehensive law. For guys like you, if we want you we *have* you, because we make one of the sub-laws and amendments to *fit* ya. We make it just as explicit as it can be put, even when we discuss it between ourselves. So it boils down to this. If we want ya we'll have ya. If we don't want ya, *get*! But if you get worried by cops comin' round at night, you'll just have to keep moving, that's all. Doesn't matter right wrong or indifferent. Right now, get the hell out of here. I don't want to *see* ya!'

Well I took things more light-heartedly after that insight. I thought if you get away with a thing, you get away with it, and if you don't, you don't. If you get arrested unfairly, is it any different from when you got the cane at school for something you didn't do? So it's always been the same anyway. You get punished whether you're right or wrong and you're always wrong so you're always gettin' punished. So why not get punished and at least get what you can out of life. Take the punishment in your stride, the bad with the good.

That philosophy kept me going for quite a long time. I didn't try from that point on to single out the law from anything else. It doesn't mean anything, when you're told quite pointedly that if they want ya they'll have ya. So what does the law matter? Because it doesn't matter what you say, they'll find loopholes and they'll pin it on you anyway.

I came to the conclusion that really there is no law. If you want to stay free it's just up to you to see that you do, but you can do that in many ways. It depends on the answers that you give. If you do get run in, use the time to find out where you went wrong, which answer you gave wasn't the right one, how you got hooked, so that you won't get hooked again. That way you're building something, a kind of resistance to the power that gets you in there. In other words you live and you learn.

The first time I ever got arrested I said the precise thing that I hadn't yet learnt, and yet I said it unconsciously. They picked me up down on the Auckland waterfront, and I was sleeping in what was a disused builders yard, just a few old bits of timber lying around, been there for donkeys' years. If had had an iron fence around it but over the years the railings had rotted and it was all falling apart. You could've driven a blinkin' bus through it, there was practically no fence there. And they had me up on a charge of bein' idle and disorderly. My first experience of it.

When I got up before the court the old magistrate said to me, 'You were found illegally on enclosed premises without intent.' Well that sounded like a lot of rot to me. I had one intention and that was to have a sleep!

And this is what I told him.

I said, 'I had every intent, sir. I was intending to sleep, until these guys came along.'

'But,' he said, 'that's not what we mean.'

I said, 'Well, what do you mean?'

'Well,' he says, 'you had no intention of pinching anything?'

I says, 'There was nothing there to *pinch*.'

He said, 'You couldn't sleep there. You were on enclosed premises and are therefore an idle and disorderly person. So we're remanding you for a fortnight to Mt Eden Prison. You'll be coming to see us again in a fortnight's time.'

Well the fortnight came and up I go again. We went through the rigmarole charge again and he said, 'You broke into this yard.'

I said, 'Sorry sir, I didn't break into anything, I walked in. If I had a team of blinkin' horses a mile wide I still could've walked in. With the horses. There was nothing else to stop me.'

'Aw,' he said, 'we checked and found that there was a gate there, and it was padlocked.'

'Oh yes,' I said, 'There was I suppose if I'd bothered to look. But there was no need to look. The whole place was wide open.

He said, 'So long as there's a gate, two posts and a padlock, that's the same as if there's a whole fence around a whole place, that's all there needs to be in the eyes of the law. And if you go behind that gate, you are trespassing.'

I said, 'Ooh well, do you expect me to carry that around in my hip pocket, a book or something, of all these bits and pieces, to tell me in everything that I do, whether or not I'm breaking the law? I can't stop and figure it out first, I haven't got the time.'

'You remember in future,' he says. 'If you do the same thing again you'll get a stretch. This time we'll be lenient.'

They've had me boiling inside at times.

You're only so-called free, by a very thin thread. People, when they see something unusual, or see someone do something unusual, become interested. They're like children, what they see they want, and if they can't have it they want to wreck it for others. They get a false idea of a fellow doing something different, succeeding and apparently quite happy. They don't realise that we all have our own personal experiences in life, and the richer an experience the more it costs.

Maybe you have to go to jail occasionally, even a mental asylum. You have to be brought to the realisation that the world is not what it tries to make out it is, some sort of righteous clean place. Sometimes it's a dirty filthy hole.

I never got into anything I couldn't get out of, and that goes for ditches and jails. A lot of what I did get into and didn't get out of is because I didn't try. I believe it's easier to wait. Especially in jails. The stone ones! But I never attempted to get out of 'em, that was too much hassle for me, although I could've.

At worst, jail was three meals and a bed. Outside, I thought, I've got to pay for it, here it's for free. No hassle just to stay alive. But you get rusty after a while and wish that you were anywhere but there. Not that a little bit of rest'd do me harm either. Might as well, since I'm here. Meals aren't all that bad, and you get a dry bed at night.

The tricks they get up to in there'll amaze you. There's not much else to do. You spent a lot of time lookin' for stashed stuff in cracks and between bricks and all sorts, the odd live match here or there, that sort of thing. Guys hoarded stuff who didn't expect to be shifted from one cell to another. Cigarette butts in queer places.

Of course in those places too, you don't know who's who. There could have been psychiatrists dressed up as prisoners for all

I knew. You wouldn't even suspect. Anyway, they were all prisoners to me and I used to talk to them no matter who they were.

I even got some released. Yet I couldn't get meself released.

I got one guy released *three times*. He was there for life, really stuck. It was a major victory to get him out *once*. As soon as he was out runnin' round he went and did the very same thing every time. He was a habitual blinkin' car pincher. He only had to see a car and he'd hop in and drive off. No sooner was he out the gate than he was convertin' them again.

So the next day he was back again. I said, 'Look, buddy, you came to me and you asked me to help you. Well I got you out, or at least you were gotten out somehow. Not you've cooked your own goose. It was hard enough to get you out the first time. Now it's near impossible. After all this time you've been in here, they've trusted you once but you made bloody idiots of 'em.'

'Oh,' he said, 'I'll never do it again.'

'But,' I said, 'that's what you said the last time, mate. You've got to mean what you say, somewhere down the line, but quick! We'll have another go and try to get you out again. But the next time I won't even try.'

Well I'm buggered if I didn't get him out again and back he comes in a couple of days. I said, 'I'll have just one more go. You'd better keep your fingers crossed. People are tryin' to help you but they've got their limitations. You've done enough pinchin'. Give it up. That's how simple it is. Turn your back on it.'

'Alright,' he said, 'I promise. I'll never do it again.'

Ah, bugger me. He got out a third time and he was back within a week. He lasted a couple of days longer this time, that was all.

'Well,' I said, 'I'm forced to make the same conclusion that all the others have formed. You're bloody hopeless matey. Dinkum. There's somethin' in you that clicks when you see a car. You can't help yourself. You've had it mate. I'm very sadly disappointed but there it is straight. Prepare for a long, long, long, long holiday. 'Cause that's exactly what you're gonna get!'

He was quite a likeable little bloke too.

I was an intermediary between them and God in that place. I said, 'Look matey, how do you think you got released? The only thing that I can say is that I asked for you to be released in a high quarter - actually the *very* Highest quarter of all. Now who is that likely to be, matey?'

'Oh,' he says, 'that'll be Mr Johnson! The Superintendent!'

I said, 'Is that the Highest, is it? Well God help us, mate!'

They put me in the asylum several times. I'm like the guy they put in the army. One fella says, 'There's only one thing wrong with you, mate.'

'What's that?'

He says, 'You're the only one in step!'

In the lunch hour you could roam freely, so long as you didn't escape the grounds. I was wanderin' around in that particular area, and there was another ward, K ward or something, where all the worst cases are. And they were all like monkeys in a cage. Big high wire fence all round 'em. And some were climbin' up it too. Some were jumpin' up and down just like chimps. Some had their legs crossed all the time, like a yogi, they couldn't undo themselves.

One guy thought he was a radio station. He wouldn't go out that door until they put a thing on his head with a big mast stickin' out on top. Then he'd be walkin' around and he'd sit down after a while and he said, 'Hello, Radio such and such calling, yes, yes, receiving you,' and he'd break out into a queer sort of song.

Well, along to me came one of the screws. 'Not a pretty sight, is it,' he said.

'No, it definitely isn't, matey. It makes me wonder how they happen to be like that.

The screw said, 'You know, when he came in here, that fella was a perfectly sane, healthy guy.'

'Oh,' I said, quietly. 'Are you really dinkum?'

'Yeah!'

'Well' I said, 'how'd he get like that?'

'Aw,' he said, 'a lot go like that, after they get in here.'

There's more to be said for the *police* than for the people who run *those* places. But not a helluva lot more.

Once or twice you get your own back. My own bloody colonel in the army, was the very magistrate who sent me up for the eight months in the asylum. Old Richardson. We had served during the war in the Middle East. Now you know what I finally did with him? I jumped on his head, not once but half a dozen times. And how did I do that?

I happened to be looking for bottles all around the back of Matamata. And suddenly, quite unexpectedly, I came upon a cemetery. There in front of me was a new stone with all these new flowers. He had only just pegged out.

I kicked his bloody flowers from here to next Christmas and then I jumped on where his head was. Yeah! Just to make sure he stayed down. He's still there, that's for sure. I made sure of that.

How could you be so fortunate, as to come across an old friend? Especially your own dear old colonel!

In recent years the cops've left me alone on the I and D thing. And it seemed to coincide with having the bike. It was potential money. Assets. And I could have a lot more assets because I could carry them.

So I piled all the sophisticated gear on it that I could, so that they could see what they were lookin' for. And they thought I was a person of substance.

Then when reporters asked me why I had a bike and I'd say it keeps me out of jail; that was the truth.

Some people looked at all my gear and said, 'Are you an artist?'

I said, 'An artist? I'm an *escape artist!*'

The Ohiwa Camp.

"I've got a pozzie now mate, aw it's a cracker. I've been thinkin' of takin' out a mortgage on it!"

Sometimes you come across places where the main road once went around every little bend and cliff by the water. Then they made cuttings through the hills to straighten the road which left some of the old cliff-hugging bits isolated. The undergrowth moves back and the forgotten bits of road get all grown over. They are like hidden little tracks. You can't see them unless you're looking.

On the East Coast there's a few spots like that, around the Ohiwa Harbour between Ohope and Kutarere. I went in one, one night, on my way round the coast and I intended staying only a night.

I ended up staying there for three *years*.

It was the ideal place to build a thing I had dreamed of with which I was going to join the caravanning fraternity. It ended up small, my caravan, about three foot by three foot across the end, and six foot long. It was in two parts, two cubes and one telescoped into the other. Going along the road behind the bike it looked like a single cube.

I made the chassis out of a car-seat frame that I found in a car down a gully and two bike frames that came from a dump. Luckily they had back wheels and tyres and I only had to purchase tubes.

It was a bit of a hassle in many ways. I knew what I wanted but I was influenced by a mate who offered to pay for aluminium for the sides. So it ended up like that, with the framing made from a dumped television aerial. But this particular caravan wasn't what I *really* wanted.

I had been walking along a ridge one day near Whakatane. It suddenly pelted down with rain and I ran into the undergrowth. I found this big white polystyrene foam packing box as big as a car case. It had a big crack in it but I went in it and it kept me dry. Warm as toast too. And that gave me the idea to one day build a caravan made of polystyrene.

In my mind it'd be all moulded in one piece, with a built in bed, cupboards, sink and windows. You'd use plastic cutlery and sail-cloth curtains. It'd be *super*-light. One day I was going to drive down the main street of some busy town on my bike towing this conventional sized caravan behind me. It could be a twenty footer or more, and look normal, with shiny fibreglass thinly coated on the outside.

It'd be *un*licensed, too.

A hell of a joke and I could do it with ease. You can imagine the looks on the faces of motorists, who'd overtake me only to find a pushbike in front.

After that I'd like to build a great big ship, build it somewhere where nobody knows what you're doin'. Out of polystyrene, but it'd be something that looks about five hundred tons! Paint her all authentically and everything and one day just go up the main street towin' it, a hundred footer, with your bike, and have a big laugh on the town.

I'd stop halfway and have lunch!

It'd be original, something no-one else has done before and absolutely practical.

With all that in mind I started collecting polystyrene as I found it at dumps. I was goin' to shape what I had into regular equal-sized bricks and glue them all together when I had enough.

Meanwhile, though, I made this other caravan. It had Perspex windows, wooden framed, opening out. The roof was gabled and along each side was guttering made from plastic hose cut lengthwise in half.

So when it rained I collected the water in buckets.

I cut a removable trapdoor in the floor so I could sit up in bed and put my legs down onto the ground. In that position I could cook, fix things, read, write letters if I wanted to and get washed and dressed.

SuperTramp

Through the trapdoor I could get in and out the caravan in wet weather without opening the front door and letting the rain wet everything.

I had me beach umbrella over the front door.

That was my veranda.

I cooked under its shelter, with my converted paint-tin portable stove. I could barbecue on the patio in the pouring rain. How many houses could you do that in?

Without moving from your bed!

One day along the road I found a half-eaten tomato sandwich. I looked inside to see why the original owner had thrown it away. There was a slice of tomato and a spot of pickle. Nothing terribly wrong with it as far as I could see. I was tempted to finish off what he'd started but I had a better idea.

When I got back to my camp I *planted* it, just to see what would happen. I figured the tomato seeds might sprout.

And sprout they did. But they came up crooked. Well I figured that was the vinegar in the pickle.

So I left them alone and watered them every day and pretty soon they straightened up. Then I picked and transplanted the young side shoots and they came up too. That spring I had a couple of hundred tomatoes to dispose of.

I was eating them like a train!

You can see that first tomato plant, comin' up behind the water tank.

So just by waiting, I ate that bit of sandwich over and over again about four thousand times.

There were wild strawberries growing about twenty miles away.

Rather than ride each week on my bike to check their development, I transplanted one right outside my caravan door in a pot. When that one was ready for pickin' I knew immediately the state of the *main* crop.

The caravan didn't move, when it was finished, although it was built to. At that place I never knew how long I would be there, it was a day-to-day existence.

I didn't live it that way though. Although a cop or the health department or someone else could come any day and tell me to move, and I was always half expecting one of them, I slowly got settled in.

I decided I'd I put in a big garden, because I had absolutely no idea how long I was actually going to be staying.

I still worked hard, very hard, what with going out for the bottles and doing the garden too. I used to spend all day out on the road getting bottles. In the end I had hundreds and hundreds of them. It took me the three years to build up a substantial reserve supply, a situation where I had about four hundred or five hundred, hidden. I put them in a bank! I called it my *reserve bank*.

When I wanted some butter, I just went up the road to the shop, with so many bottles.

Normally the bottles would travel from Ohope to Opotiki – the camp was between these towns - and that's half of them because I only did one side of the road coming this way, but by that time I had half me load. I still had to go home to Ohiwa. So on the way back I did the other half and I arrived back with about six dollars' worth in one day.

I travelled from Thornton to Torere and back in a day, two thirds of it on foot, and got back between sunrise and sunset. I was in bed before dark.

It's like havin' a bull behind you, you can run twice as fast when you have to, and I was determined to do it. And until I had me reserve of bottles, I felt I couldn't sit back. The pace was hot, really hot. I was exhausted, but still I ran along.

Initially the ground was hard from being an old road, and there was gorse everywhere, great big roots of it. I had to grub them all out first before I could even get to the pumice.

I made little paths in the camp by pressing every inch of the pumice down with my thumb, skimming everything off level and filling bits in here and there. It ended up dead level right through.

It got like concrete.

I placed bamboo sticks in the ground around the caravan to make a trellis for beans. Then I interwove a thatched roof.

It actually went all leafy and luxuriant, growing into itself. It became a *living* shelter.

SuperTramp

I had bench seats for visitors, made of planks I found on the road. Cauliflowers, cabbages, onions, tomatoes, broad beans, they all did very well there. I only had a short time to build that ground up from zero, to producing great crops.

But it was twelve months before I even ate a good spud, mate. I had to survive all that time and do work that I knew that I was going to get little reward for.

I didn't even know that I was goin' to be there for twelve months! I didn't *ever* know when a cop was goin' to turn up next. So all my work might've been worth nothing. But I went ahead and did it.

Spuds, I had them in rotation, a continuous system, working like clockwork. As I ate one row, there was another ready for planting and another ready for reaping. And one went in as quickly as one came out. Bet your boots on it.

All hand-mulched, gathered from nature itself, no unnatural

manures - just dried grass, buried. When I put in a row of spuds I put in a row of dry grass on the bottom. Always. All the ground did was support the plant. It was pure pumice. So you *had* to put the spud's food in first.

I used to use my own toilet waste diluted down instead of super. But vary it. A layer of that and a layer of soil. Human fertiliser has to be well composted before you can use it because it is very acidy.

So my first source was hay, because it was clean to handle and there was plenty of it.

Of course, when you first put the spuds in, one of the very first things you do is saturate the ground. Because of its porous nature I needed a barrier to stop the water draining through the pumice.

Black plastic again. Strips of it from the tip. Not covered all over, just lengthwise along the spud's row. This allowed a certain amount of the water to go down, but not all of it. It also made the spuds grow quicker because it held the heat longer in the ground.

I even had to produce me own *water*. I found a place where there was a fissure and from it I got a well. I dug a big hole in the papa rock and that acted as a tank. It filled up with beautiful crystal water.

I had a chute, and I used it to water this way and that way, and I had a system of alternate irrigation. The water used to run along the rows.

I put in about an hour of that every day, haulin' water up by hand.

It got really dry from February to April. After that the rain took over again.

I conserved the water by not feeding the roots but rather, feeding the foliage.

More effective too. Just pour it over the leaves. It works for all vegetables, probably all plants if it comes to that. Especially veges, though, because they're leafy things, and there's more area that can absorb the moisture.

In the end it was all garden, from the entrance to the wagon near the cliff. Onions grew along the path and the tomatoes were up there in a big patch. Some wild carrot heads were at the very edge. I now produced *all* my own vegetables and fed several other families as well - the oyster farmer and his wife at the entrance to the Ohiwa and Odette over at Ohope.

At the road entrance was a huge wattle tree. The telephone people chopped it off because the branches hung over a wire. I was never short of firewood, and I had it all cut *for* me.

The path to the camp started from just the other side of the wattle, and once clear of the tea-tree, the garden started on the right. Right from there to the big pohutukawa was all garden, about twenty metres.

But from the road you could see nothing, just an overgrown gap where the old road had more or less been.

One day there was an electrical storm, and the next morning I found I had a new spring of water coming out of a fissure in the bank. It was the day Snowy#1 disappeared, too, and a bit of a slip came down off the cliff. Whether or not he was under it I don't know. I never dug to see. I couldn't bring myself to. It's better the not knowing either way. It wouldn't have made any difference.

But he never came back so that leads me to suspect that he might've been under it. He used to like sittin' over there. I think he used to do some fishin' of his own from that spot when I wasn't watching.

It would have slipped right away where he was sitting. Then again he could've taken to the bush. He was free to come and go as he pleased. There's another two cats buried over there anyway. Old Ginge and Snowy#2.

I never paid for a thing there, in that garden. The old shovel was one I found ages ago on a tip, no handle, just a stump of a shaft. I dug the *whole ground* with it; you wouldn't believe it was possible.

I found an old file on the road, and I kept the blade sharp when I was digging. But man, the work that thing did!

I got all my seed spuds off a tip too. A whole sack of 'em! Rua seeds, really good. Somebody just chucked it out! I got it all together again, put it into another bag, and away I went. I carried it all the way from Taneatua, over the hills, and there was about, oh, eight great big pumpkins on as well that day. I had called in to the Whakatane tip and found plants and pumpkins everywhere. I couldn't see me leavin' them behind so on they went.

Fifty bottles as well.

All on the bike, mate. As well as, oh, numerous things I picked up along the way. Even firewood, a special type that I got from Ohope Beach. Full of saltpetre. I went home loaded like a donkey every time I came back.

There was a little plum tree, there was a peach tree. I even had a hot-house, plastic-bag lined. There were mussels and mullet down there. And plenty of punga close at hand for stews. I was well set up.

One day just like any other day I came back loaded up and happy in my heart. It was a bit breezy but that didn't matter. I was looking forward to getting' home and putting my feet up. As I got near the entrance something crossed my mind and I hesitated. To this day I don't know what it was or why. But somethin' wasn't quite right. Maybe some undergrowth near the entrance was disturbed in a way that I wouldn't have done. But I entered a bit carefully…

I couldn't fathom it. Vandals had been in.

I was disappointed because at that time there was a fair bit at stake. I'd chosen well. The place was unused. Not inconveniencing anybody. It'd been unused for years. Now at least it was supporting one person.

There was no point to the damage. Anyway I fixed it up alright. It took me about a week. Then you wouldn't have known they'd been in.

Plants were flourishin' then. It was just about at that three year stage when the ground was nearing perfection. That's how long it had taken me.

Everything was all go. And I was still building up my reserve bank.

At the end of the week after the damage I went out on the bike pickin' up bottles. I had about six dollars' worth on board. It was just about sunset when I neared home. Was I hungry! I was going to treat myself to a bit of stew, bake some scones, and maybe cook up some pikelets to have with blackberry jam.

But I was tuckered out. I pushed the bike up the path and around the long shelter of the toitoi, into my hidden camp.

I looked around and blinked. I thought for a minute I was in the wrong place.

Everything, but *everything*, was *gone*. Flattened. Burning.

They'd uplifted my wagon and tossed it over the cliff, along with trellises, seed boxes, you name it. The garden looked like a herd of cattle had barged through it or some sort of bomb had dropped. Plates and tools and bits of ripped plastic were everywhere. Branches were broken and left hanging. More than half my bottles were smashed too. In the middle they'd set fire to my bedding and the clothes.

Some of the vegetables were nearing harvest. *All* of 'em had been pulled out. Uprooted. The ripe stuff had been pinched.

I looked over the cliff. There it was, the remains of the wagon, all twisted and tangled in branches half way down.

I just looked around. It was gone and finished. Three years of it.

I didn't know what to think. I wanted to just walk off.

But I didn't leave. Yet.

First I cleaned it up. The whole place. There was nothing to force me to do it. But I did it because wherever I camp I always do that. Even if it was only for one day or night. It took me three days. Then I walked out.

Once I left I didn't go back. No point in going over old bones.

Sure my heart was heavy.

But everything passes. At least I'd had three good years.

And I told myself, just another page in the book, matey.

Fishing

"I don't eat pipis now. I let the fish eat them and I eat the fish."

Some of the local Maoris around one place tried to get me out of my pozzie where I always went fishin'. They set logs afloat so that my lines'd be carried away.

I just went on fishing.

In the end they got tired of it. All the logs just went out to sea.

It was playin' dirty, as far as I was concerned. I wasn't harmin' them.

I used to go down by a bridge over a river. A few kahawai made their way up there to spawn. Suddenly a whole truckload of Maori people'd turn up, *just after I got there*. It happened three or four times.

They'd get out, two gangs of them, with nets. One'd work the downside of the bridge upwards and the other gang, up from the bridge downwards. They'd meet in the middle, bringing everything into one place; *my* place. But I never saw 'em catch a fish there yet, not one.

Just went there to give me aggravations.

As soon as they all packed up and went, I was catchin' fish. From the moment the people moved off, the fish started rollin' in.

Some Ministry of Works guys were workin' on a bridge over a river. They were chuckin' off at me as I was fishin'. They were hardly workin' themselves. The Lord spoke of the Ministry and he spoke of works, but he never mentioned the Ministry of Works.

I could hear 'em laughin' away in the shed, havin' their lunch. Just before lunch I got a couple of little tiddlers and oh, that caused great shouts of laughter. They made suggestions about a long time in one place and catchin' damn all. Over lunch they were enlargin' on it, you know.

So I packed up and went down to the river mouth.

I came back about an hour later with a great big twelve pound snapper. A real beauty.

I hung it up on the bike, on a pole, and I drove past all the graders, all the bulldozers, everything. How do you like that, matey, was the message for all to see. You know, this old guy, who wouldn't know anythin' about fishin'! Did I have some fun!

Dead true.

Then along they came.

Oh, *very* curious about me now. This fella, must have some mana or somethin'! He might have somethin' that we haven't got.

The local Maoris do come along occasionally to watch me fishin'. They wanna know how I get it, what I use for bait, how I'm doin' it. And I don't try to hide a thing.

'What'd you get today mate?'

'Oh, the day's young yet matey. I haven't started yet. I'm only preparin' still. Later.'

They've never seen me catch one, a decent sized fish yet. They know I get 'em. But they don't know how. And it's got 'em buggered.

I don't know meself really. I know a few things, but not much. I know it's out of my hands, largely.

One guy told me a feasible yarn, yet a bit fantastic. He said 'What would you do if you had to get a duck, something for your tea?'

I said 'Well, most likely I'd ride me bike.'

He said 'But how would that get you a duck?'

'Well, it could happen, a car could go past and knock one, it might even land in me lap. One's been pretty close, a pheasant it was.'

'Oh,' he said. 'Not sure enough,' he said.

'Well,' I said, 'how sure do you have to be?' When a duck falls in your lap there's nothin' surer than that mate.'

And you know what he said to that? He said 'I'll tell you a Maori way.'

'Oh,' I said, 'that'll be interesting. I've heard all about the Maori one. I wonder if yours is the original.'

'Yeah,' he said, 'it's the right way. What you do is find a drain. And when you see some ducks you let 'em land in the drain.' (He didn't say where they were coming from or anything) 'When they land you drive 'em up stream. If you keep driving them far enough and slow enough, eventually they'll go up 'til it narrows down. If you go right to the end,' he said, 'it gets that narrow they go in there and they're too long to turn around to come back.'

I says 'Look matey I may look silly but where did that duck come from in the first place? That's worse than ridin' bikes! First you gotta find that kind of drain. Then you've got to wait for that duck. Then you've got to find one to be in the right position. Eh? It's a bit fantastic!'

This is what he didn't tell me, how you do that. It's easier to ride the bike up and down the road and wait for one to fall in your lap!

You hear some beauties on the road.

These duck methods can work, any of them, but they don't. I've even tried to trap seagulls, I've been that hungry. But it can never happen unless it's meant to.

And it's the same with fishing. The other day when I was down there I caught this great big two hundred pound stingray. He hauled me down the beach for about half a mile and nearly into the water, too. Eventually he straightened the hook out and he got off.

I fixed the hook and re-baited it and then in half an hour he was on it again. He straightened it out again but this time not until I got him on the beach. The hook just dropped out of his mouth as I got him clear of the water. I believe I was meant to catch him.

You don't have to buy gear. I go round the high water mark after storms and find hooks and things washed up, so by the time summer comes again I've got a whole set of gear. And I don't fish round rocks where I could lose it.

So I've got a line now, it's in five pieces, and I've caught more fish with that line than with all the rest of me sound lines put together. It's just got hooks that I found on the beach. And I can throw that line in anytime and within minutes there's a fish on it.

It's supersensitive. It's the combination of different gauges of line in conjunction with different resiliences. Somehow or other, unbeknownst to myself, when I strung that line together, I came up with a line that fish can't resist. It's nice and springy and I think when they bite off it, it really fascinates them. When they're bitin' they're not muckin' around. I always wondered why this line caught fish so quickly. I didn't know I had what I did. Now I know.

Once a farmer on a hill saw me muckin' around on the beach and came down with a shiny flash rod in his hand. 'Here you are,' he said, 'I've been watching you and I thought you might be able to make use of this.'

I looked at it. It must've been worth a hundred bucks. I said 'What do I want that thing for?'

He said, 'Go on, take it. You'll catch more fish.'

I said, 'Well, what do I want *more* for? I'm catchin' what I can eat now, with this hook and bit of string. And there's always pipis if I get hungrier. Anyway, besides all that, I'd have to carry that awkward thing with me.'

Well, he went off home, he just lived on the hill to the back of the beach, and he took the expensive rod back with him. But he was a kind-hearted man, he came back later that evening with some vegetables for me. He said, 'At least you can carry these inside you.'

One way to fish is to just camp beside some guy who owns expensive gear. Admire all his paraphernalia and get into talkin' with him. Pretty soon, a fish'll come.

I've got fish off the road, mate, more than I could ever eat. Here I was, just out of Tauranga, and I came across this Maori guy fixin' up his roof-rack.

I said, 'Oh, what's wrong mate?'

'Aw,' he says, 'me rack's worked loose. And I haven't got a spanner.'

I said, 'This is your lucky day mate. What size'd you like?" And I pulled out me toolbox and gave it to him. They were all off the road, bits and pieces that I'd found over the years.

When we'd finished he opened up the back of the van. I've never seen so many fish in one van. All in sacks.

'I'm takin' these to the pub,' he says, 'to sell 'em. Here,' and he put three into my arms. 'Tell you what,' he says, 'take a whole sack!'

I said, 'What'll I do with a whole bloody sack? It'll be all me and me cat'll be able to manage just eatin' one!'

I'd never got as many from the sea in one day as that guy offered me from the *road*.

Quite a few times when I was fishin' off the beach, really big fish'd come and break the line and tow it away with all me gear. So I invented a fail-safe method.

I nicked a groove in the top of a seven foot long stick. Then I shoved the stick upright into wet sand, down about eighteen inches. I laid a big bit of driftwood on the ground beside the stick, at right angles to the beach, so he's facin' out to sea.

Now I bait my line and throw it in. I take the line comin' up the beach and pass it through the groove then down beside the stick and wrapped a few times around the seaward end of this driftwood. From there the line is tied to an anchor log, further up and parallel to the beach.

When a big fish takes the hook he pulls and one end of the driftwood lifts up a bit. The other end stays on the ground. This weight supplies give and play in the line.

In an emergency you can flip the line off the groove. This

gives 'im more line instantly and lessens the tension so the hook doesn't straighten out.

I've found all the weaknesses in the system and the answers to the weaknesses. And the beauty of it is, it all comes off the beach, the whole lot of it. Even the bait, everything. Even the lines.

There is no fish I won't eat, even ones many people seem to disdain. The porori is a beautiful eating fish. He'll come to anything smelly and one of the things he likes best to eat is cow shit. Yeah! Open him up and that's what you may find. But he's a nicer fish to eat than snapper. More moist. And he's a vegetarian. He doesn't go eatin' his mates like a kahawai.

All the fishes that the Maori say don't eat, they're the best matey. You know why? The same reason that they call porori the shit-fish.

It's so the pakehas don't eat 'em!

You ask a Maori about porori and he'll turn up his nose. You ask him where the best pipis are and he'll say over there. Well, you say, what're you gettin' 'em *here* for?

I've had pipis give me a crook back. They affected my spine. They were semi-poisoned. The local Maoris only gathered theirs from well downstream, but they don't tell the pakeha that.

I told a Maori chap one time something he'd never heard before. He said to me, 'Do y' eat pipis?'

I said, 'Yeah. Only Maori ones.'

He said, 'Why Maori ones? How can you tell a Maori one from a Pakeha?'

I said, 'When you see a lot of Maoris, that's a sign. When I'm in a hurry for pipis, and I wanna get the best, I don't look for pipis, I look for *Maoris*. And when they've all got their heads down I know exactly what they're doin'. I know *why*. I know where the best pipis *are*. I know the best way to *get* 'em. I know the tide is just right and it's the right time exactly, to the minute mate, I know the *whole* story.

But I don't look for a pipi one iota. I can see a Maori from a mile away. I can't see a pipi from an *inch* away. Put that in your blinkin' pipe and smoke it!'

Next time I saw him, oh about a year later, he got me back. He came saunterin' over and said, 'Saw you down there gettin' pipis today.' I said, 'Yeah, that's right.'

He said, 'Were they Pakehas or Maoris?'

Here's how you use pipis to the best advantage for catchin' fish. You put them into an onion bag and take 'em over to where there's a decent-sized log and you bash hell out of the onion bag on the log. But you only do it so much, so that the pipis are just only just broken, enough to let the aroma out of a few.

They float to the outside of the bag when they get to deep water, and the fish just swarm around it. There are various versions, you can even tie hooks to the onion bag.

Christ said cast your bread on the waters. There were some fellas fishin' when he said it. It's a strange thing, but bread is a favourite food with a lot of fish. You have to really roll it between your fingers so it goes back like dough a bit, or like plasticine. It sticks on a hook too, pretty well. Certain fish go for it more. Mullet go for it like bloody mad. Snapper, porori, trevally, are all keen on it.

But actually when Christ said 'bread' what he meant was, feed the fish and they'll feed you. In other words, all you have to do is use the fish to feed the fish.

Then cut his head off. Don't throw it away. Put it in a bag and keep it fresh. Do that by digging some dry sand away and stick it in the wet sand. Bury it, if it's a hot day. All the offal and that, put it all together. And then, before you go, put it into an onion bag and chuck it into a certain place in the water, a place where you can take a bearing on.

When you come back the next day, the offal will still be there and there'll be fish all around it. Now, if you continue to do this thing, oh for a week of two and then start fishing, well...you'll see the small fish go around it and they bring the bigger fish. The big kahawai comes around chasin' the sprats which want that offal and stuff.

Cast your bread upon the water. The very fish even, that you would otherwise throw to the seagulls or something. There are many ways of ground baiting and of them all I think pipis are the best.

Where I fish is generally in the mouth of a river and there's plenty of rip there. But it's not there all the time, only certain times of the tide. I know what these times are and I'm waitin' for them. I know when it's possible to fish and I know when it's a waste of bloody time. The tide can be quite different from hour to hour.

But you'll never know this unless you fish there consistently, and keep your eyes open to see the subtle changes in the directions of the currents, the incoming tide flow and how that changes. The reason for this is that you've got one lot of water opposing another.

So it's a continual battle. Now, just before they're actually in balance, the rip slows down, actually because one is balancing the other. If you wait until it's dead flat, this'll be full tide.

Another way to tell is that the wind suddenly drops. The tide pulls the wind in, it must be friction or something. You get a big blow, then suddenly, nothing. That's the turn.

You could miss gettin' anything, for the reason that it's a shade too late. The thing is to catch it when it's not perfectly in balance - just before that, while there's still a bit of flow. Then you'll be bang on.

So you can spend the whole day fishing, and only a half an hour's actual effective fishing. The rest's just a waste of time. You'd be better to stay at home and do some other work and then go.

Sometimes there's preparatory work to be done. I might have

to be at a certain river mouth at seven in the mornin', to get me pipis before the tide starts comin' in. At times I've had to get bottles, fish like mad on the way, get the odd vegetables, sometimes fruit and quite a bit of it, cash the bottles, mostly on foot, and be back again fourteen kilometres, before sundown in time to cook my meal before dark.

Sometimes you can't see how you're gonna do everything in one day and yet you will, but how are you unless you plan it ahead. You say, oh well, there's no time left for fishin' because it takes say about half an hour to get there. It's time-consuming before you've even got a fish.

On the incoming tide, they come in like armies.

They come in an order. The first ones are the wee smallest fingerlings kind of, called smelt. Little wee tiny sprats and baby mackerel. They're more like whitebait in a way. Then you've got the small wee herrings. Then you got the bigger ones, then the bigger ones, all comin' in one behind the other. When they've been up the river, some of them have spawned, the big ones.

The last ones that came in, these are the ones you get, just before the river balances. But you should be well prepared before that.

When I go fishin' I don't believe in goin' fishin' and paying for fish to catch fish. Not ever. I go empty-handed and I come home never miss, except on one or two occasions for the whole season, and that's bein' out there practically every day.

We're talkin' about days, month in and month out from

November right through to at least the end of May. From there on it's a waste of time. The water's too cold and everythin' else. So you give it up, and grow a few more cauliflowers instead.

When you're fishing you've got to keep everything open. At times you've even got to fish with your big toe! As a matter of fact I've half eaten a fish before he's out of the water sometimes - one line in that hand and there's a fish on it, one line in this hand and one line in me mouth, in me teeth. I play the one in me teeth by just keepin' moving backwards and forwards.

I'd be sittin' down opening pipis and at times the fish're comin' so thick and fast that I can't keep up with them. So I just half-hitch the lines around me big toes. When I get a bit I jerk my legs. So I fish with me feet too. That leaves my hands free to prepare bait.

But your fingers are the most sensitive. You can feel what kind of fish it is by the way he bites. In fact sometimes you can tell precisely when to give that jag, if you're goin' to give any at all, by just feelin' what he does. Especially with a flounder. He's a tricky beggar.

And you have to keep your *ears* open. The messages come from the most unlikely sources. Messages from God above, I mean. And you've got to use all your powers of discernment.

You might have heard people say, 'Aw, I backed a winner,' or 'I just had a hunch.' It wasn't a hunch at all. That's a worldly term. They were told to do the thing and they did it and they won. They could be tellin' you, 'Look, you've been catchin' mostly mullet. What about a bit of snapper for a change?' By just something they say.

It might come as, 'Do you ever catch a snapper here?' And I'll say, 'Oh yeah, I've caught one or two. They're not thick and heavy, by any means, but they're there, sometimes.'

Then they go right off that altogether, onto some other subject and this gives you room for thought. Why were they so pointed about catchin' a snapper? Then you try something, that generally would catch a snapper. Switch your gear, put out another line that would more suit one. Different bait on it. Chances are very good that it was the message. You won't know for sure until you've actually caught your fish.

'Here's class so-and-so,' a school-teacher came up to me once and said, 'and they all want to catch a fish. Could you show them a few tips?'

I said, 'More likely, if I tried to, they'd start showin' me a few. No, I'm not bein' caught with that one, that's old hat. I'll tell you what I will do, matey, I'll tell you one thing they're doin' wrong for absolute certain, and it can be changed in seconds. Listen - you don't catch fish on dry land, mate.' Here they are *sittin'* here.'

I turned to one boy and said, 'Matey?'

He said, 'Yeah?'

I pointed to the water - 'That way! Not here! You want to catch a fish? Not here ever. There!'

Did he go! He thought I was bein' smart but it was the truth.

Soon as I said that, though, he thought all he had to do was throw his line in the water and he'd get a fish, see, just because I'd said so.

That's only the beginning. At least now it's in the right place. He'd been runnin' round in circles gettin' nowhere. Yellin', and full of enthusiasm. The look on his face was fantastic, when I told him to go to the water.

I said to the guy, one of the teachers, 'Did you ever think you've got to have your line in the water first? I can't see any blinkin' lines in the water.'

'Oh,' he said, 'They had 'em in there.'

'For how long?' I said.

'Well,' he said, 'one or two of them, for a minute or two.'

'If you come down here,' I said, 'and expect to get a fish in a minute or two you need to start givin' lessons in patience. That'll do them more good than all the fishin' courses in the world. Let 'em learn a few of those things first and then send them fishing. They want a reward for nothing and they want it quick, when they say. Aw, quick, out with the flash gear, down to the water, it's all on. Next thing, they're dejected, ambling back up the beach with their gear, with their head lookin' beat.'

Then they came up to me and said, 'Hey, you've got fish there, but you haven't got any line in the water.'

I said, 'No.'

They said, 'Well, why do you stay here?'

I said, 'I'm waiting for something.'

They said, 'What's that?'

I said, 'The fish. I'm not fishin' when they're not there, I'm waitin' 'til they get there. Then I'm startin' fishin'.

They said, 'How do y'know when they're there?'

'Aw,' I said, 'easy. I know by the tide when they're there. To be sure, though, I start fishin'. When I get a bite, that's all I need, just one bite, then I know they're there. if I get a bite reasonably quick I know that they're thick. If it takes a while for the bite to come I know I'm just a shade early as yet.'

The odd occasion, and it's very odd, four times last year and only once this year, do I completely miss catching something. And I suppose it should be like that, missin' occasionally, to keep you on your toes.

To keep up interest then, you don't want to catch 'em so quick. You want to find means of *not* catchin' them like that, to keep the unpredictability and the striving level up, the uncertainty.

I know that there are really two fishermen. One is you and one is God. I catch the fish, that's fair enough, but I don't put him on the hook. He puts himself on. I can go a long way towards gettin' him to put himself on, but the last word is with God himself.

Everything you killed was God because he's his own creation. When you kill a fish you're killing God. He knows beforehand that he's got to die, to keep you alive. But since he's in you too, then he's dying to keep himself alive, because when you eat him that keeps *you* alive. So when you kill, you also create and sustain life.

He might even want a little joke.

Goin' fishin' you know you're up against something you can't beat. You could scotch the idea about God and say isn't that what you had to do anyway? Because it is. But the knowledge of having something greater to fight besides the fish makes it all the more acceptable and more liveable and interesting. Now you know that you're not up against the fish and yet you are, but when you know who the fish is then you know better who you're against, or who's the other player in the game. You're tryin' to win a game that you cannot win, and yet you must play the game otherwise you miss out on fish.

It's all fun and games.

I tell 'im so sometimes too, I say, 'Hey, you're not playin' cricket! You've straightened out that hook! I had you fairly and squarely hooked!'

Then I have to think again. Maybe I wasn't discerning enough, in my buyin' of the hook. Perhaps I should've taken a pair of pliers with me, turned me back to the guy who's got the shop; and to see how tensile the steel was, should've tried to bend it.

I've even had them talkin' to me. And yet not them; you could say once again, God. Because once I caught a fish who came swimmin' up to me, goin' round and round, tryin' to tell me somethin'. I thought I must've got a drunk one or something.

I used to fish at a certain spot by a wide river mouth in the sea, and I caught lots of mullet. I could catch 'em pretty quick there. As soon as the locals found I was catchin' fish they got their nets and raked them in. It just dropped right away after that so I took it in me stride and I didn't fish there anymore. These things more or less happen. I thought, well, I'm gettin' a wee bit tired of mullet now, so it's time to have something better. A kahawai'll be alright.

Then I saw this great big old man kahawai coming down the river, like a bloody shark, on top of the water, swimmin'. He was only goin' slow, at a friendly pace, didn't seem to care about me or anythin' and I thought, crikey, I could just step in and lift you out of the water matey.

And that got me thinkin'. I suppose if I step in the water, it mightn't be so easy as it looks. So I won't be doin' that. All he's tryin' to tell me is, soon you're goin' to catch a big kahawai. It mightn't necessarily be any particular kahawai, just a kahawai. And I thought, well, keep fishin'. Sure enough, within ten minutes I had a kahawai. And it wasn't him either; it was a shade smaller.

I said, before the first one had got out of sight, oh easy, anyone can step in and grab that, but then I counted that from experience things have a habit of not bein' so easy as they look, and so I might've got a duckin'. That was not on. Also he might've been a sick fish, and I'm not gonna take advantage of a poor old sick fella. So I let 'im go.

Later I thought, maybe he wasn't sick, he was only tryin' to entice me to get a duckin'. Maybe he'd've swum clean between my legs and stuck his spines into me along the way. Put me off balance or somethin' and have me flat on me bloody back into the water.

I need fish for my cat. But just to be there, is worth going. There is sufficient solace out there in the place and the activity, in the certainty of success and the enjoyment of the whole day.

But it's more than the being there, it's the being privileged enough to be able to be there, that is something in itself. Especially when you see that you're the only one there. In the early morning, before the heat of the day, when you're out in the open and not in a smelly tin box, that's the best. And you're on the road or the beach and open to every sound there is around, birds and whatever else there is but a motor.

A man says to me, 'I drive past here every day. I drive one of the big trucks. I see you sittin' there, but I never see any fish. How the hell do you do it?'

I said, 'The thing you should be lookin' for is the reason that you never see a fish. It's because you're goin' too fast.'

A couple of Dutch or Germans came along once, one was a pretty girl. She came to me with a very inquiring look on her face. I had just caught a huge kahawai before she'd got there and there it was lying all beautiful and shiny.

She beckoned toward the sea. 'Did you get that out of there?'

'No, lady, no.'

'Where did y' get it?'

'Up there. Look. See that cloud up there? Just to the right. Look about two degrees to the right and that's where it came from.'

She didn't get the message. She didn't look offended in any way or feel she'd been had. She didn't turn a hair. And the guy was standin' there looking on with a big grin on his face.

But then in that moment I saw the sea in a dimension that only happens once in a while, and I did something that was quite out of character in a sense, at the time. Just the sight in front of me made me say something that was unrelated to fishing, really, but made me feel a deep appreciation deep down.

I knew I gave that couple a jewel, and yet it was God, because I said to them 'Never mind that down there. That's dead. Look that way. Look at that beautiful water!'

And it was fantastic that day. It was alive. Somehow their presence drew my attention to it.

'Isn't it beautiful,' I said, 'isn't it fantastic? It's really something! Isn't that appealing?'

Well look, they just got a few yards from me then they stripped off and into it. I had passed something to them and they had caught it and leapt in swimming on the strength of it. They had no idea of doing that 'til I mentioned it. And I had been sittin' lookin' at the sea all day and not noticin' how beautiful it was.

What they saw is what I saw, an extraordinarily beautiful sight of an extraordinarily beautiful sea, really special. And I knew I'd given them something. A little hope too, because I think they were a little browned out about things. They'd been walkin' down the beach lookin' for something - well they found it, when they got to me.

And whatever it was, it was right there in quantity that day. It was super. I went in that water myself after them and by crikey, afterwards I went like a bomb. I packed my bike and cycled home like crazy, back before I even knew it. And I had a lot of fish too. It just electrified me and I know it did the same for them.

Well what better could you give a person? Hope too, where they though there was no hope. Now they knew that there was something a lot richer than what they'd seen before. Because the scene meant a lot more to them, if only for a moment.

I think they saw something that they'll remember for the rest of their lives. They'll have to connect it to something supernatural. They'll be lookin' for more of those moments when they go to the beach again and I hope they see it but not too often, or it'll lessen in importance.

So there's no need to give a person anything, in fact you can give without knowing sometimes. Like the one who said to me did you ever try usin' a smaller hook? He gave me something, and that's a fish.

But he didn't know it.

SuperTramp

Finding Food

"You take an inch of fennel stalk and soak it in water overnight, then add baking soda, sugar and tea. In the morning, try it. You've made Coca Cola, no question about it."

A grocer once asked me how I managed. I told him, 'Oh, as best I can.'

So he said 'But what if you didn't have money for essentials like flour and fat?'

I said 'I'd eat non-essentials.'

He said 'But what if they weren't available either?'

I said 'Well it's still no problem.'

'Why, what would you do?'

'It's easy,' I told him. 'I'd just go without.'

This is probably the best meal you could ever have. The one you don't have. The one you go without. That's a spiritual meal. When you've had a few of those you're so much better off when food's not around.

Then again, if you need more than bread and butter you're not really hungry. Because when you're really hungry, man, does bread and butter taste good! It's heaven. It's all you want!

If you choose to fast, the desire to eat disappears in a couple of days. If you don't choose to eat you may choose to die. Starvation is quite painless if you choose it, but if it is forced upon you, the mind'll make it a horrific experience.

Once I found the remains of an elderly Maori in the bush who'd clearly planned his own death. He was stretched on his back in comfort, within handy reach of water and food. He took less and less of it 'til he died. Perhaps when I'm ready, that's what I'll do. It can be viewed as a thing of beauty.

On the road you learn to conserve, recycle, and get economy of movement. I learnt a few things in jail too, in that line.

For instance that if you dry tea out again thoroughly, it all shrivels up again and can be re-used, rejuvenated.

They only gave us tea once a week. Then every day we got a cup of boiling water and they said make your own tea. So we used to put it in a piece of toilet paper and sleep on it. It got itself dry overnight. Next morning we had the same tea again. It still had as much taste and colour.

Travelling, at one stage I had a system where I used to have a big bowl of a special mixture. From that I could make any number of different things. It was basically a sourdough culture.

I could make bread, pancakes, all manner of sweets, puddings and fritters, by takin' out some of the mixture and treating it in any number of different ways. If I put little bits of bacon in a portion of it, the yeast would absorb the flavour and the whole thing'd taste like bacon. So I'd get a hell of a lot out of a little.

Then I'd put a bit of onion in another one, or some cheese. By adding a little wee minute piece of anything and lettin' the yeast do the rest, then deep-frying, I'd get beautiful savouries.

Then I'd grab some more of the culture, add it to a bit of flour and milk and up would come nice bread. Once a week I added a bit of milk powder, gave it a bit of a stir, and left it. Once a fortnight a bit more salt.

Before I left each morning I just put into a bowl a couple of tablespoons of sugar and added as much flour as the amount I'd taken out to cook with the night before. It had to be kept wet and it needed sugar each day. It was carbohydrate, that's what it fed on.

You didn't have to use it every day if you didn't want to. You could leave it a month.

You came in tired and hungry, both, extremely so because you hadn't eaten all day and you been workin'. You travelled a long way. You'd been over hill and over gully and down dale, in the raw and on the road. But you still had to eat. So to come to a bowlful of stuff that you could fry up immediately, was nice.

All you had to do was take the top off the bowl and put a spoonful with its additive into the pan of boiling fat. What you added you stirred in gently, and with loving care, or you might frighten the yeast to death.

And this is how you make it, startin' from scratch. Two or three cups of flour, add and mix in a bit of sugar. Use salt water or milk and add some 'til it's not too runny and not too thick. Get four small potatoes or one large, cut into four. Peel. Put the whole lot together. Leave beside the stove. Don't cover it up. In five to seven days it's ready for use.

At the Ohiwa camp, I discovered the simplest system of all. It was a pancake that could be made with just flour and seawater fried up. So all I needed to carry was the flour. To give it a bit of a nutty taste I got hay and chopped it up real fine, then added it to the flour and water. Hay and grass is, after all, just another variety of wheat, just wild grasses.

You make your pancake and roll a pipi in it. That's dinner. Make another one and roll a fruit in it and that's dessert.

I met a drover driving cattle along the roadside and I ran and picked up a handful of hay lying near the road before the cattle got to it. The drover said 'What are you doing with that?' I pointed to the cattle and said 'I'm just gettin' my lunch before they get theirs!'

At the moment I'm using a new recipe for bread. My cat prefers it. Two and a half tablespoons of bran. Eleven tablespoons of flour. One third teaspoon of salt. Five teaspoons of baking powder. Half moderately heaped tablespoon of sugar. A level tablespoon of milk powder. Mix in a liquid to make a dough. Add a couple of teaspoons of butter. Bake half an hour.

Many a time I've cooked without a pot. All you need's a paper bag. Or a plastic yoghurt carton. Fill it with water and suspend it over an open fire. The thing won't catch fire because the water inside keeps the temperature down to no more than a hundred degrees. So you can make tea in a paper bag. That's a tea-bag!

One of my earliest experiences using plastic sheet was when I was comin' up from Gisborne one day. There's a crayfish shop on the right hand side just before Whangara. I was goin' past, and a fellow just at that moment came out the shop. He said 'Hey! Hey! Hey!'

I said 'What's the matter?'

He said 'Come in matey, come in. It's blowin' a bit out there. I'd like to talk to you anyway.'

I said 'Have I done anything?'

He said 'No, I'm just interested.' So I talked to him for a while and he was interested. He asked me why I was doin' it and a hell of a lot more. But he seemed genuine in his interest. He was a patient listener.

After a while I said 'Well matey, I'd very much like to be able to stay and talk to you for a long, long time, but I'm afraid it's getting on, and this is one time that I have to be particular that I'm in bed by dark. So I'll have to move along because I don't know this part of the coast so well that I have a place to know of, to camp down readily. I have to start lookin' for somewhere a bit earlier than usual. It might take me a while so I have to make allowances for it. I'll have to say toodle-oo but I'll be coming this way again and maybe I'll give you a few more minutes of my time and enjoy you're company. I'll see you again.'

Just as I got out his shop I heard 'Hey! Hey! Hey!'

'Yeah? What's the matter mate?'

He said 'Come here come here, it won't take a minute.' And he opened up a great big coal box freezer. 'Help yourself. Fish.'

'Eh?'

He said 'Pick out what you want. Plonk it on the counter.'

I said 'I haven't got any money mate.'

'Oh,' he said, 'I'm givin' it to you. Treat yourself as my guest and accept this as a gift. But put it on the counter.'

So I did, and he wrapped it in newspaper and said 'That'll keep it fresh 'til you get where you're goin' to cook it.'

I said 'Cook it?'

'Yeah,' he said 'How're'ya gonna cook it?'

I thought that was a funny thing to ask. Yet he must've been a pretty observant guy because I was travellin' light then and he seemed to appreciate that I hadn't a plate or somethin' to cook it in. When he gave it to me, he gave it with the palms up, like it was a special gift, almost in a religious sense, and not just any old fish. This struck me oddly. I'd better think about this, as I'm goin' up the road, along with the other things I have to think about.

How does 'e know I haven't any gear to cook it in, 'cause he's dead right, I haven't. It could be a messy business and I haven't cooked a fish yet without any utensils. I haven't any fat, for a start. I haven't even a fork to eat it with.

So I went along, thinking, and when I got to the sand I dug a couple of holes, built a fire in one, waited 'til the embers went down, and I thought, why are you doin' all this? Anyway, you can get warm while you're thinkin' of it. Of course it's to cook the fish, but where do you go from here? Here's your fire, there's your fish, cook it! Then the crunch. How?

Suddenly there was a hell of a bang, just behind me. It interrupted my thinkin'. It made me look in the direction of it. I looked and found that I was lookin' out to sea.

Now I thought, what the hell happened? There was a helluva loud bang out there a minute ago, but there's nothing out there that could make a bang. No ships, nothing.

It was a special wave, it went off like a whip. It happened in the right moment, to attract my attention in that direction. I hadn't figured yet what it was, but having turned in that direction I thought I'd better turn back. As I did, my eyes dropped to the sand in front of the fish. And I saw something, some seaweed. There were three lines of it.

When the tide comes up it deposits it. Thoughts started to dawn on me. The highest line is the driest. It's had time to dry in the sun. The next lot is half dry and the next is dead wet. I knew that seaweed'd burn like anything so long as it was really dry. So I just hopped out the hole and grabbed an arm of the dry stuff and set her alight.

Burn? Wow! It's full of saltpetre, that's what they make matches out of. I piled it on 'til it finally smouldered.

Then I thought, well that's impressive but it doesn't solve all your problems matey. It's a helluva lot of *heat* though.

I looked back to where that wave made that crack and then back at the seaweed again, and I noticed that the next lot of seaweed was just a bit wetter.

Finally it came to me that if I put some of that on, and damp the fire a bit, and then put real wet stuff on top of that, then put the fish on top of that and more wet stuff on top of that again, I got a hangi.

An open air one. A new kind, *one the Maoris never knew about.*

It went up like a geyser when I put the wet stuff on, a helluva cloud of steam. For the cookin' I only had to wait about five minutes.

Then I said to myself, how do you eat it, get it onto somethin' without it all fallin' apart? Then I thought, you don't. You leave it right where it is and you pick at it. With your fingers. That's your fork. And the hangi is your plate.

That was my first real appreciation of having little. No pot, no plate, no knife or anything. If it hadn't been gutted, I couldn't have even gutted it. Although now I would've looked for a good sharp shell. But at that stage I'd had enough hassles without muckin' about thinkin' how to cut it up or fillet it or something. I didn't disturb it at all.

And I found I could eat every skerrick of it. From the top down. When I got to the bones and backbone I just picked 'em out and sucked 'em. Then I ate the next half.

He warned me to start thinkin' now how to cook it, because there'd be little time once a camp had to be found to give it any thinkin' time then. By the time I got to the beach I had one or two tentative ideas but nothin' final. So God thought he'd shoot things along a bit, and that's when he cracked his whip!

It's the simple things that've been worked and worked to your advantage that have been the most priceless. Like an infallible way to build up a fire in the pouring rain. And you could sit and enjoy it with the storm lashing about you in the middle of the night, pitch dark except for the fire and warm as toast drinking coffee. You've achieved something.

I've seen myself run down the road flat out in the middle of just such a night with the rain pelting down, just to keep warm. I left all my gear behind and running not only to keep warm, but to keep warm whilst I was looking for an old piece of car tyre, or tube, or both, or one of those plastic ice-cream things, all fuels that will burn in the rain. They're all made from oil.

The one starting at the bottom is the plastic bag. I used to light the lip of that and it burned very readily because that's mostly candle-grease. Then I put a piece of car inner tube on top. That'd catch fairly readily providing you had sufficient heat under it. Anything under it had to be nonporous because if it soaked water it'd go out.

So you had the plastic that would not soak water then the inner tube that would not soak water, then you had your tyre which was the finishing touches, and all for free and all readily available on most sections of roads.

It could turn what could've been a very uncomfortable night; if not near blinkin' death possibly from exposure; into something really pleasurable. There'd be just the umbrella up, the fire out the front blazing away like nothing on earth, the wind blowing the smoke the other way and enjoying it brewing up, even baking bread on some occasions.

People have asked me this and that and sometimes I've been happy to explain things. But sometimes not. I often think that when you're in that situation you'll discover what to do *yourself*. And I tell them 'I'd be robbing you of the joy of that if I told you now..'.

But some things you only discover by chance. Like how you could make smoked fish on toast *without smoked fish or a toaster*. Because I made that more than once. And I didn't understand how it worked for a long time. But now I've got the whole picture on it.

I'd be on the waterfront, in the middle of the city, right next to the footpath. People were comin' and going. I would make toast using the toast as the walls of the toaster. You stack four pieces like a house of cards, each leaning on the other. I made a small fire in the middle out of pieces of newspaper, handkerchief size, crumpled up. The lid of the fire was the bottom of me billy, which had water and tea in it.

Now what suspended the billy? I had a forked stick, and the fork went through the billy handle. The stick was about three foot long. I sat cross-legged with the setup on my right. The forked end of the billy-stick went over my right thigh and the other end went under my left thigh. By raising or lowering my left thigh, the billy raised or lowered over the fire. On top of the fork was resting your fifth piece of bread. So that billy was your damper, your heat regulator, and your pot, all in one.

You kept turnin' the toast around to do the other side or replacing it with fresh bread once each piece was done. On the path in front of you was your pile of bread, a pile of dry crumpled paper pieces and next to that, another pile of wet ones. By adding the dry or wet I could regulate the flame inside. And I got a taste like smoked fish!!

But I didn't have a bloody clue why.

But years later I was in a library, looking up some weeds I had found that were edible and I thought I might be able to match them with known families of vegetables. I stumbled onto a description of newsprint manufacture in Canada. Apparently fish oil is used in the process. A light went on in my brain. So that's it matey!

You've waited all these years, and that mystery is now solved. Somehow the fish-oil taste must be released when you burned that wet newspaper.

I wouldn't go anywhere for just one bit of food, wherever I went there'd be possums, rabbits, all sorts all over the road. I never went wanting for meat. But I wouldn't kill needlessly. I wouldn't go out and shoot a great big deer, just to take a steak out of it and leave the rest there.

I don't pick unnecessary vegetables either that I can't eat immediately, unless it's for convenience to save myself a huge hike every couple of days to where it's growin'.

There'd be wild raspberries, gooseberries, pumpkins at Ohiwa, wild tomatoes, pumpkins at Matata, and potatoes at Awakeri, in their hundreds. Some market gardeners must tip rotten lots over banks or something, because I've found the other side of banks covered in vegetables.

In fact people don't use vegetables properly. You can make a cabbage last a long, long time if you want, and right down to the last bit. When a cabbage goes off, usually the rot sets in from the outside or the first three leaves or so. You pick it up and it's all sort of slimy, but inside the heart's alright. When you start eating it, peel off how many leaves you want for each meal. You don't ever cut that cabbage. You just break leaves off at the base, leaving the plant in the ground.

So peel off the slimy leaf, then the very dark green one - he's a bit bitter - and the *next* one, slightly paler, is the one you eat. Now even if you've got a whole row of cabbages, keep going back to the one you've started 'til it's eaten. After five or six feeds off a cabbage you're down to the last little bit, like a cricket ball. Break it off and eat it.

I don't uproot anything if I can help it. When you just cut the side leaves above the ground, you're really pruning, which does the plant good, and the next time you come around the plant's still there, so you've got a constant food supply.

As well as cauli and cabbage and broccoli, you can just take the leaves you need from lettuce, mint, and silver-beet. And if you cut the cauli head off and leave the rest of the plant in the ground it'll even grow a new head.

It's just your method. You don't need fridges at all, if you live by one rule, which is don't take any more than you need for the day. Perhaps the time you spend, if you're a conventional person, to accumulate enough money to buy that fridge, could allow you more time to do gardening and not need a fridge. There are plenty of ways of finding that time. Gettin' up a bit earlier, perhaps working a little later.

When the Chinese were runnin' the show as far as vegetables go, they knew how to dress a cauli. They didn't used to cut the leaves short as they do now. They used to leave the right length of the stuff that's useless to leave on. If you strip the foliage of each leaf on each side, what you're left with is a stick like celery. It's sweet, bloody beauty! And the centre - the stalks of the flower itself - it's the best part!

But you try and tell 'em. Try to tell a woman what to do in her own kitchen.

By crikey.

I always like to have a certain few growing things around me or with me, especially some onion, mint, parsley, and rhubarb root,

With the rhubarb leaves you're never stuck for a pudding or a fruit taste. And do they grow! All year round, those things, because you're just eating the foliage. There's no waiting for something to get ripe. It is a fruit yet it grows in the manner of a vegetable. You can make a jam with it, stew it, make a pie, blend it with apples: it's very versatile.

If there was too much food at one campsite I might bottle some or make a jam, especially if there were wild raspberries around. Then I'd hide them so that when I came around next time, there they'd be.

Sometimes I put seeds down, like tomato, knowing that I'd be coming back two months' time or even five months and I'd look for them and have a good feed. Sometimes they didn't come up at all. Things like pumpkins keep on growing themselves, because the thing rots and the seeds grow inside and use the mush to live on while they're growing.

I planted a lot of taro up around Hicks Bay. Each one has got a lot of little bumps on it. Each one can be cut off and planted individually and you can still eat the original vegetable, which is as big as a turnip.

I treated taro as potatoes and mashed them. Superb. And the next best was taro chips. Just like the real thing.

I didn't even have to dig 'em. They were growin' everywhere. And I'd go up the road further to catch a fish, so within the hour I'd have a good feed.

There were all sorts of varieties but one patch was clearly superior to the rest. No other clump was quite the same. I decided that sooner or later I was goin' to eat that lot out. So I took plenty of bud bits from it to plant out. I stuck 'em everywhere, in conditions I knew they liked. So they should've multiplied like mad. I won't know 'til I get back up there.

I even made my own flour out of taro. Grate it first then dry it. You can make beautiful ginger cake with it. It came out better'n bread.

There are three ingredients for good cooking. Bulk, taste, and eye-appeal. It's no good workin' all day findin' your tucker only to see it go in one delicious mouthful. Then you're not gettin' paid properly for your work. Number two, if it *tastes* rotten you'll throw it away whatever it is. And if something *looks* terrible you're not goin' to enjoy it no matter what.

It took me a while to cater for eye-appeal. Bulk is easy, I use a lot of punga and tree fern stalk and that's growin' everywhere. Taste, well, you can always add sugar, blackberries, or some other fruit.

When I first cooked with taro, it looked purple. There's not much food that looks purple, mate. In fact, purple is the very worst colour for a food. Then I just waited around wonderin' what I could do to improve the situation. Pretty soon I got really hungry and me guts started scratchin' on me blinkin' backbone. By that time it was dark and I couldn't see too well.

I tasted it again and I thought, gee, you know, it's not that bad actually. Then I ate it. It was pitch dark by now and it tasted blinkin' fantastic. I couldn't see a damn thing!

That was my first real lesson about the need for food to look interesting. I figured there must be all sorts of ways to set it up.

One way, if you don't like the look of a thing, is to just not look at it. Turn your head the other way, shut your eyes. Or you could do it with different bits of coloured celluloid with the sun shinin' through it making the colour go on your dinner. You could have any coloured dinner you liked then. You could swap 'em halfway 'round if you got bored.

In the wild, there's all sorts of things to live on if you have to, if you know what to look for and where to look. There are certain pointers that point to where things are. You *know* stuff is at hand or it isn't. Instinctively or spiritually. You don't have to cover acres of ground lookin' for it, like some of the Maoris do with puha.

There's some reliable signs. A group of circling seagulls can lead you to a pumpkin. Why?

Because if they're circling inland, it's likely to be for only one reason. They're over a rubbish dump. And there'll always be a pumpkin somewhere around a dump, especially an old abandoned one. Possibly also a potato or two.

You see, every town has a tip. Every town has a greengrocer. Where does that greengrocer dispose of his rotten stuff? In the tip! Then the council bulldozers turn the soil over, to get rid of the stench. This creates compost. Things grow through again, in the best soil there is!

Look for a crop of macrocarpa trees and you'll generally find mushrooms nearby. Roostin' shags are an indication that the outgoing tide is turning to incoming. They're gettin' ready for a sprat lunch'.

Sometimes things are even sign-posted for you. How easy it can be. Like this soda-water fountain I came across, up north around Kerikeri, right beside the road. It was just bubbling out of the ground. I emptied me water containers and filled 'em up with the soda. Then believe it or not further down the road I found some lemons overhanging from an abandoned orchard. All I needed to add was the sugar. It was a real hot day, and I sipped cool lemonade all along that road.

There's very little in the way of plant food that you *cannot* eat. But some have a season, and sometimes it's only a particular part that's edible. Potatoes for instance. Cattle that eat the leaves have died.

And the poisonous plants; well they can be used as purgatives.

For a long while, if somebody told me a thing was poisonous, I would immediately try it, just to prove them wrong. Often they *were* wrong.

Sometimes they wouldn't want you to camp there and they'd tell you the water was dirty. I've drunk millions of gallons of this so-called dirty water with no ill effect.

If people believe something is crook, for them it definitely will be crook. And it will definitely affect them adversely.

Most people are walkin' on good tucker all the time and don't even know it. Like dandelion and plantain and thistles and puha. They're all related to spinach. You can eat clover too. Especially the stalks. It's got a pleasant tang to it.

And there's a nice grass called soury grass. It tastes like rhubarb, with an acidy tang. And daisies. And nasturtiums.

Nasturtiums have a beautiful tasting flower with a nectar box full of sweet-tasting juice, You can eat the leaves too, and the seeds, which really become capers when you leave them in vinegar. That's all capers really are. I remember being told in the old days that chewing grape leaves quenched your thirst.

A lot of these things are *weeds*. Really, with a lot of people you wonder if it's worth tellin' them anything. They go away thinkin' you're a damn fool. 'What's'e want to eat weeds for, when he can eat apples?'

Well, they don't know the secret. The thing is you don't eat weeds all the time, only in necessity, and this is when they taste the best. Because you're more hungry.

People go to all kinds of trouble pulling out weeds by the truckload and taking them to the dump, paying for petrol to get there. All they have to do is leave the pile where it is. They can mow over it. They mow their lawn. That costs them money.

They miss the benefit, that is available and free but they hate the sight of - that's the lawn clippings. It's nitrogen and of the highest quality.

So now it's in the dump. It makes the very best compost. It's a bit sacrilegious.

There are many edible weeds that are a nuisance to farmers; wild onion for a start. Ask the farmers. They're only too glad for you to come and take their wild onion plants away. They come up in the middle of the fields and the cows eat them and it taints the milk.

You can take notice of the farms you're passin' and what they're growing. Also the wind direction. You can work out where the wind would've blown seed to and walk on the road accordingly. And there beside the road you'll find crops you can harvest for nothing. They're growing on *your* land now.

Most motorists wouldn't notice. They pass too fast. They don't see individual plant's, only farmers' rows. I take note of what the rows consist of and then start lookin' beside the road for the same.

The birds help too. They see a bit of turnip seed. People sowin' it, so they have a feed. Then they'd have a bit of a fly and look for some freshly dug ground.

They'd want a worm to go with it now so they'd go to something like an embankment on the side of the road, by some road works. This is freshly dug. And by big machines. All those guys are workin' for ya. And for the bird.

So he flies from here to there and has a bit of this that and the other. And he has a shit at every stop.

Well, all the seeds come out of him and later sprout and along I come.

So we all have a damn good feed, for nothing by all accounts, while the guy that's plowin' the ground is gettin' paid for doin' quite a different thing.

I was coming down from Auckland and I got as far as somewhere the other side of Whakatane. I'm buggered if all down a bank and up near a bridge there wasn't these huge bloody swedes. I just got me bike right down to the bottom of the ramp and parked it by the guardrail. Then I walked back. And there was about half an acre of blinkin' huge juicy ones. So I got down amongst them.

The most I could carry was what I'd got already, only three, that's how big they were. I thought well, if it's gonna be three, these are double normal size so I'll get really big ones. That's worth six of ordinary size.

And while I'm pickin' I'll eat one too.

That's a harvest of seven. Eight if I'm eatin' *two*.

Then I started to leave. But before I got away, a Maori guy drove out in his car from a house which was on the other side of the road.

He stopped below, and the next thing, I saw the fella come up, as I finished makin' my selection.

I didn't know what his hassle was, because I was on public property.

He came up to me and said 'D'ya like turnips?'

I said 'Heh heh, you watch me mate. I'm only lookin' for the very best though. I'm particular.'

He said 'You might as well. They're mine' .

I said 'Come off it. This is not your property.'

He said 'No. it's not my property, but it's my bloody seed! I got a helicopter to sow the seed and the wind changed. And it all came over here. You might as well help all-and-sundry to eat it, 'cause they've all had a go!'

Actually he turned out to be a very nice chap.

'Look,' he says, 'I wouldn't begrudge you a thing. I like your style. I wish there were more like you. Help yourself.

They're all yours!'

SuperTramp

Accidents and Illness

"One guy said 'What do you do if you get crook?' 'Well,' I said, 'I suffer it to the utmost matey! And when it's impossible, I go the other way, to get a bit of relief!'"

When they said aren't you afraid of gettin' sick I'd say 'Not a bit. I'd just lie down and stay there 'til I got well. I'd make myself as comfortable as I could.'

I'd know exactly what to do because some time ago I was sick. Way down in Hawkes Bay. I saw a side road and it was a hot day. There was a big grove of macrocarpas alongside this boundary fence. And it looked like a pretty quiet place to me. It was just a metal road but the trees looked inviting to be under, especially on a hot day. So I thought I'd go down there and have a rest. Away I went.

I parked the bike and put down me bedroll. The bike was parallel to the road making things a wee bit more private. I didn't bother puttin' up the umbrella, though I had it then. So far so good. Me bedroll down, all ready to have a rest, but I'm gonna have a feed first.

I sat on the bed and I boiled a billy on this little kerosene primus that I'd started usin'. I had the water ready.

Then I happened to look to the left and I saw a whopping big mushroom. Big as a dinner-plate, under this macrocarpa. And I'd found mushrooms before under macrocarpas.

So I went over to have a look at it. The top looked okay, the underneath too, although it had a slight tinge of just-off pink. And it had a thinner stem than I'd seen before. Somehow I felt not quite convinced of its edibility.

I looked around me to see if there was any more but there wasn't. I knew then that it was the crunch, I was gonna have to eat that one.

I decided to cook it. I made pikelets with no sugar on. I brewed up again. All I had to do was cook the mushroom in a bit of butter and eat it in sandwich style between pikelets.

Anyway it was poisonous. It laid me flat. Crikey, within half an hour I was paralysed.

Yet I'd done some homework without realisin'. The bed was already made and I was sittin' on it. It was just as well because I couldn't move. I could only lie in one way without any pain, and that was flat on me back.

I was under the tress so the sun didn't affect me. But something up there drew my attention. And that was hundreds of sparrows, nesting. And they were chirpin' and makin' a helluva bloody racket. Like they were arguin' all at once.

I thought gee, what makes them so blinkin' happy? Then I thought oh yes, nesting time. It took me out of meself and helped to ease the pain a bit. And I thought, you wouldn't be so happy as you are if you were me right now. I began thinking, oh well, they're just another living thing, just like me, I wonder what they'd do in the same position?

There's such a thing as doctors for us but not for a bird. Maybe they'd just rest. I had to think, if somebody stops, a car or something, and asks questions, the next thing I'll know is that I've landed in hospital and in all sorts of captivity. So if anyone does stop, I made up my mind to say that I was just resting.

But I was thinking too that a bird'd do only what a bird can. It can fall out of a tree and land on the ground.

What then?

If you are a bird within minutes or hours you could be there with your legs stickin' up in the air, dead as a dodo. Could a bird do anything about it?

He'd just take it in his stride. He doesn't need to think about when he gets sick, he doesn't even know what death is. And his mates around him haven't got a clue either. If he stopped chirping I don't even know if they'd wonder why. He just crosses his bridges when he gets to them. He'd do the only thing you could do.

And this is wait and see. Stay where you are.

By midday next day I found that I was alright.

These were simple things, but very valuable things, that you learnt through simple things happening, like when they put you flat on your bloody back, unexpectedly, and in a position where you had to look and listen and ask questions why and how.

If you could solve them for the birds, you could solve them for yourself. After all, they're just loners. Just smells, just eyes, ears or nostrils, blood and guts, nerve, muscle, gristle, just the same as you are.

A little thing like that and here's this almighty man, so knowledgeable, so big so proud. Yet the bird'll leave him for dead.

One time my back gave out at Waiotahi, and I was sure it was after eating poisoned pipis. I took off to Hikuai on the other side of Opotiki. I just couldn't walk any further. I just managed to get there, and my bloody back felt broken. I had to crawl 'round the bike to get the last few things on it.

At Hikuai I got a big fire going with four logs around it like seats, in case visitors came. I didn't have to get up to feed the fire because the ends of another four logs poked into the fire and they just had to be moved into the flames as the ends got burnt. If I happened to have visitors I made sure I sat in the middle of one of those seats, and the visitor was in a position to push logs in. Also, bein' in the middle meant I could swing my legs up onto the log and lay my back down on the other half so I could rest if I wanted.

I was so totally immobile that every movement was murder. I planned everything so I didn't have to move too often. It worked admirably. The only crunch came when I had to get four more logs to fuel up. Crikey, it took me all day to get *one*.

I said to myself, God damnit, me of all people, here I am livin' on my own and I can't even move. Right next to a public road.

And I've been here for nearly a month now and people must be really startin' to take notice. People're gonna start askin' questions and the moment someone says I'm crook, the next thing I know, the cops'll be here, the ambulance and God knows what and it'll be everything but what I want.

I had formulated in my mind what I was goin' to do. One night after dark I was gonna start *crawling*, mate, to get away from that place. That was gettin' close. Each day was gettin' nearer to that time when I'd be down that road, leaving everything back there, on my hands and knees, because I'd made up my mind nobody was goin' to make me get me off the road for anything.

But I'm not waitin' forever. Only so long. If something doesn't come up soon, the deadline's not far off and I'll start that crawlin'.

It turned out that I didn't have to.

'Oh,' he says, 'You've got a nice fire there, do you mind if I join you?'

I looked up and there was a guy standing there out of the blue. I hadn't seen or heard him coming.

I said 'Not a bit, mate.'

Then we got to talkin'. He said his name was Sayer, and he was an osteopath, so I said to him what the hell's that? He said

'Well, bone trouble or muscular trouble, sometimes I find that I'm able to put it right.'

He looked more like a clergyman. I thought, this must be a true experience from the Lord. He knew I was crook and that I'd never go near a doctor. He knew just the man to send to cure me.

'Who are you? I said. 'A tourist?'

'No,' he said. 'I live here. I have a practice.'

'Aw matey,' I said, 'you're just the man I need! But quick. Are ya any good?'

'Oh,' he said, 'Most people think so.'

'Alright then. My bloody back's killin' me matey, and I've been stuck here for a bloody month nearly, and I don't *want* to be stuck here. Fix it, mate.'

He said 'Alright. Just lie down on the seat here, tummy downwards.'

He fished in his pocket and he came out with a bit of copper wire. He pulled my shirt up and my pants a bit down and he ran this wire up and down my spine. When he got to a certain point he said 'Do you feel this?' And it was like a prick. Did it hurt? No. A little bit further down, same thing. He put the wire back in his pocket and used his thumb to push on me spine.

'Oh,' he said, 'you're very fortunate. I can fix you with ninety nine point nine percent surety, almost immediately, but time and rest'll do the most. I'm goin' to push with my thumb and when I do I want you to arch your back.'

So I did and I heard this click. I told him and he said 'Yeah, one of your discs were out. And it's your diet that did it to begin with. The gristle in the disc has been caused to harden. To complete the cure I'm giving you the vitamins you need. I'll bring you a mouthful.'

The next day he arrived with two beautiful big pies, home cooked, an apple pie and a steak one.

'Here,' he said, 'take these, they're a couple of pills for you.'

I said 'They're a little bit on the big side aren't they?'

'Well,' he said, 'they're full of vitamins. Just what you need. Eat 'em.'

I said 'Man, you said a mouthful!'

I've watched the animals lick themselves. That works well for small cuts. Your saliva contains antiseptics, antibiotics and sealing compounds to stop bleeding. Who knows it better than the dog! Saliva is always with you, you can't lose it and it's free, a never ending supply. Of course when Christ fixed one man he spat in his eye! And that healed him, gave him eyes to see. It could've been the shock!

Someone wanted to check me teeth, and I said no, check your own. Don't tell me what to do with my teeth. Same with me eyes. Any discomfort would suggest I shouldn't be readin'.

One thing I can't work out is how come when I want to hear someone talking I can't but when I don't want to hear a motorcar I can hear it from miles away? I thought once, someone's puttin' one over on me! But I suppose you only hear what you want to hear. It can be embarrassing.

Before I went out on the road my eyesight was good. But when I had stayed out for a long time I noticed my near vision was fading and my long vision was gettin' stronger. I probably got that way lookin' into the hills and into the distance.

Once I was hit by a car. Just the once. I used to push the bike up the Ohope hill on the Ohope side once a week. I would do it for one reason: so I could read at night. Why?

On the bike wheels I had hub dynamos and rim dynamos, a total of eight. They were all connected through a diode to a motorbike battery. When I'd walked to the top of the hill, I would turn around and got on the bike and coast all the way back down with all the dynamos zinging! That charged the battery right up. All I had was a flashlight bulb to use at night by my bed, but it was enough to see and read by. That supercharge gave me light for reading for exactly a week.

On one occasion I had reached the top and had just turned the bike around. I started my downhill run. All my dynamos were switched on. A car suddenly came out of nowhere and made a U-turn. Bang! It hit me!! The next thing I knew I was sitting on the gravel, badly shaken.

Fortunately, I only broke one bottle.

Ken Ring

The Way of Life

"The world is my church and life is my prayer."

One time up the coast I made a windmill, because the wind was blowin' and blowin' and it occurred to me to utilize it. I fastened a motor mower wheel to the centre of an old circular washing machine lid and cut vanes in the lid. It was ideal because it was made of thin aluminium.

I bolted one of my dynamos off the bike to it, with a bracket I took from the panniers. It had a rectifier too, it was well earthed. When I rigged it up, a little torch bulb switched on when it was going. Sometimes it lit up the whole bloody country! Goin' and goin' like nobody's business.

Now to find out where the wind was most constant took me about a week. From the north came problems, and not only wind. The best position was a knoll of rock over the road. But there was nowhere decent for a campsite on that side.

So I said, here's the problem. How're ya goin' to get the wire across the road? I racked me brains over this one for ages. You couldn't string it across, cars had to go past. And this was after all the main road 'round the coast, State Highway 35 . And you couldn't make it high 'cause of cattle trucks.

What then?

Simple, but it took a while to achieve.

I chipped a very narrow channel, about a half an inch wide in the road, right across. I had to work when there was no traffic. I couldn't let anyone see I was choppin' up the blinkin' road. So I did a lot of it at night.

Then I lay the wire in and covered it back, filling it in with stones and earth. Nobody knew. I bet it's still there!

One thing I learned on the road was not to get too set in my ways. If I needed a solution, not to make it too permanent, improvise, make it workable, and it doesn't matter how perfect you make a thing, you can always make it better. Perfection is in one thing only, and I'd spend a lifetime looking for it. The most you need is workability.

Things of the spirit need not come from discomfort. They can come from comfort too. It's up to you to sort out the devil, with his tendency to temptation, and what is some sort of helpin' hand from God.

I was just startin' goin' up the steepest hill on the East Coast on a burnin' hot day. I was off and pushin' the bike. This Maori chap stopped at the bottom with his tractor. 'Shove your gear in the bucket and hop on,' he said, 'and I'll give you a ride to the top.'

'Look, mate,' I said, 'I appreciate the offer. But if I was do so, every hard hill I would come to hereafter, I'd be lookin' 'round for a Maori with a tractor.'

'Well,' he said, 'I'll tell you what. I won't see you suffer, I'll help you push the bike!' And that's just what he did, right to the top.

Left his tractor at the bottom and went back for it later. Talk about a kind-hearted fella.

Sometimes you can be quite mistaken about people and what their intentions are. Often there's just a hair's breadth between interpretations. I find myself switchin' right 'round. And most of the time you seem to be mistaken anyway.

Your only true guide is your intuitive sense. And you have no power over that whatsoever. You can feel it in your heart whether you're doing the right thing or the wrong thing and if you feel it's wrong don't do it. Never do anything in doubt. It's better to do nothing.

If you're happy then there's no need to change your life, it's acceptable to you. But if you're not, and it's not, then you must start by cutting your bridges behind you.

You'll only have to do it once.

After that it'll be done for you and there's no goin' back. Because you've realised you're weak and you know your weakness, you've put yourself in a position where you cannot go back. *Then* you'll find you can only go forward. This is what *makes* you go forward. It's hard to do.

If you ever get on the road, you're never goin' to find Utopia. Because that's just the carrot in front of the donkey's nose - it's always just ahead. The more you find, the more you know you have to find. But along the way you're findin'. And you're doing original things.

But when you sell your life for a dollar, the boss is running your whole life for you through that dollar. You know your potential, and your potential is your real wealth.

Once I thought the greatest thing a man could do was to become a millionaire. It used to be the havin' everything, not the getting. No, that was too much like hard work! Ooh no, the having, the having.

I used to gamble heavily. I wanted to win a double every day. No matter how many I won it was never enough. Donkeys' years ago I got thirteen doubles in eleven weeks. I would think to myself, well, what a bloody fool you are mate. And I was always unhappy and miserable. Because I would think, as I got to the tote window and collected five hundred pounds, crikey dick, why on earth didn't I put another fiver on?

Now it's easy to become a millionaire by becoming a pauper. You work just for the sheer sake and joy of working. Mod cons are not appreciated at all. In fact it can be paradise doin' without them.

If life is too humdrum, it's easily altered. Throw away your bankbook for a start, that's one way. If you can't do it that way then put your money on fixed deposit for a long, long time. Forget about it.

When you discard your continual accustom to money, you'll be forced to do things in different ways. That's the key to it all. You won't become a bludger just to make it easier for yourself because you're going in the opposite direction. And you'll find you have a bank account of a different kind. One that can't be overdrawn.

I believe this world is given to us free. God never intended that we should have to pay for everything. But since man took money on as bein' a false god, God said to him, here you are, alright, buy your own. If that's your god, help yourself.

If you look at things in a monetary way, all you'll do is unsettle yourself. Money is a robber. It takes away the real and good power which is the power to get along without it. It'll only give you the power to do things in set ways, not unknown ways. When you want to find something new, that is unknown, you must do without it.

Oh, you say, crikey, I'd starve. Well, maybe you would for a while. Maybe it wouldn't do you any harm. Maybe it'd give you a healthier brain. Maybe it'd clean out your system a bit. Maybe it'd all add up to something in the end. Maybe it'll be a sacrifice, a challenge, a hard tough road to hoe, but maybe it'd be worth it.

I need to be at the helm of my own life. I've never lived with a woman although I've come close, but I rather think I'm better off by myself. I need to do all me own driving. And I'm a good driver;

that's what gives me a good life.

I've relatives that married, successfully too, and brought up a large families. But I've overheard a few rows too that probably did their bit to put me off for life that kind of caper.

As soon as a man gets married, in my way of life he'd have to get two bikes. For me there wouldn't be the same joy if I had to do it that way. That gear of mine is mine, it's original and I'm the only one that can make it work. I'm the only one who could ever know the true joy of it because I'm the only one that'll ever experience it in that way.

The big thing with me in my life, it doesn't matter whether I'm here out on the road or whatever, I'm still me. I'm livin' in myself. I'm not dependent on the world for my life. As long as I feel happy in my heart. And I do, generally. Until some rat-bag comes along and upsets the apple-cart.

I like all people really, but there's not many likes me. Whether it's me that's at fault or what, I couldn't care less, because there's not much I can do about it. I've got to face the situation and hope they'll go their own way in peace and I'll do the same.

Years ago being a loner. appealed to me as being my ideal life. A life where there'd be nothing unnecessary, where I wouldn't reach out for anything if it was six foot away. I would make it three first. In other words, I can reach anything almost from where I sit, both in my tent or caravan. I might have to put my feet on the floor to cook a meal but that's about it.

I don't believe in unnecessary movement. When I move from one place to another I subconsciously reckon, do I have to move that far to get from A to B? Do I have to take so many strides?

This is because you've got such a zest for life. You're not wasting moments. By the time each day comes you're exhausted at the end of it. But if you found it was necessary, you could go on.

After a while you realize some people around you don't even know they've *got* a spirit, or if they have they don't seem to use it much, so they don't know much about its potential.

You have to use a thing, to find out the answers. You can climb up to heaven, it's said, with a ladder, but you cannot. You can only get so high, until you get to the top rung.

But it's easier to climb up to heaven by coming down the ladder. Only by going to the top and finding that heaven was further away than you thought, it's not 'til you come down the ladder that you realise that heaven was at your feet before you went up. But you had to go up to find that out.

If I see a new road I like to go down it, to see what's at the end. And that became my philosophy after a while, seein' something through no matter what.

I took something on when I started this way of life and I have to see it through. It was never courage, it was necessity to live on the road. And an experience that got better with time. I was having a kind of spiritual awakening and I found that this was the very type of environment you needed to attain it. So I was in exactly the right spot to be buildin' somethin' real, whereas before I was only a carpenter!

The only thing I didn't much like was that I began to see that each successive challenge was getting tougher than the last.

I came to the end of the line once or twice, thought I couldn't carry on, but when I looked back on it, I only thought I had. I've been so depressed I've just sat and cried, when everything seemed so hopeless.

But you can't come to the end of the line. It's an impossibility. You can arrive at a situation where you think you are at the end of the line. The reason is that you were brought up conditioned to a stereotyped way of life.

You can only go so far in the stereotyped life before you *do* come to the end of the line. You become a carpenter and a good one. That's when it gets less interesting. It's while you're *learning* that it's interesting.

I believe God said to me, Why should I do anything for you? My argument was that although I turned my back on him it was done in innocence and lack of understanding.

On the other hand, when I thought I was doing what he wanted, what I found occasionally happened was that I wound up in jail. And that's hardly heaven.

My way of seein' God is just the same as a person, in other words just the same as you or I. He can be angry and happy. He can make us happy and we can make him unhappy.

Once it was a beautiful day, and I felt I had so much, and it was weighing on my heart. It had to come out. It was pressurized, a kind of a joy. The pressure of it pushed my hand out, to put it all in God's hands.

And that's precisely what I did. I didn't feel anything except in my heart. But when I looked along my hand, I was pointing at something that I should've seen a long time before but had never done so. A beautiful apple tree with beautiful apples on it. On this hot day it was a beautiful sight.

Just behind me was a stone cold waterfall coming down to the edge of the drain by the road. Man did I cool off! I had just came away from the waterfall and felt so invigorated I couldn't help it, my hand went out like that. What I saw of the apple tree was just the very top with a couple of apples, that was all. I was amazed. It was standin' on a near perpendicular bank, with a hell of a drop down below it to the sea.

Well I got some apples off it and it made me marvel because I couldn't really explain to anybody what put me hand out like that. Because it felt somehow drawn out there. I suppose it was a kind of reaching out to touch what I could see.

Little did I ever realise in my many times walkin' past that spot that by walkin' a couple of steps closer to the bank I could just about reach the top of that apple tree. When I put my hand out, I believed it was to *God*, in blessing, for the privilege of bein' able to *be* there on such a beautiful day and witness such a beautiful view.

You don't have to move your lips to form a prayer, or get down on your knees at all. You can say it in your heart. You can do it as you're walkin' down the street with your eyes wide open. It's being thankful for all the good things that you have.

Any other visible form of prayer is just in the imagination of man. He wants to show others how holy and righteous he is by going down on his knees.

I went to church as a child because I was made to. And I kissed it farewell. As an adult I went off and on, more out of interest than anything. Also, they gave me dinner there!

Sometimes also they showed free pictures on a Sunday. It didn't become really real 'til I made it a personal thing, until I began to meditate for myself, learn through myself, and fathom things out for myself, to test them myself. A gradual thing.

I believe God sets a challenge. He wants you to beat him. he wants to be able to say 'Look, I'm proud of you mate, you really pulled out all the stops this time. But I got one or two yet!'

It's all in fun, but so long as you keep doin' your work you'll be rewarded. So will he, because he'll be thinkin' up ideas, of how he can outsmart you again. He'll never allow you to think that you're smarter than him.

I always found that if you drop something it hides itself. So I find solutions by not lookin' too hard. If you've lost something, the best way to find it is to forget it. Then you fall over it.

At times he'll say What're'ya gonna do about this one mate? Here's one for ya. Solve that one. This is a beauty!

You get tricked into puttin' all your heart and soul and wastin' all your blinkin' time tryin' to find somethin' that you'll probably fall over later. So the same rule still applies. Forget it.

You can't though. You can only put it at the back of your mind, and he makes sure you don't forget it.

It took me thirty-five years to give up nicotine poisoning. It took away a lot of my senses, it upset my whole digestive system, it robbed me of smell, my eyes went almost blind, my hearing's had it. Not only because of that, but smokin' accentuated it. I gave up not long before I went on the road. It was a terrific battle for me but I won the day mate, I won. And it gave me the courage to win other battles too. Having won once, matey, I knew it could be done.

It's like, goin' out on the road itself, you don't know what's ahead of you and you're following a little wee spark of light. You find something that's of real use to you and it costs you nothing for once in your bloody life.

Well, you want more of that lot!

I used to walk thirty miles a day. Then I was always sorry because I had to stop. That's fair dinkum! I always felt sorry. Why did I have to stop? Because it was now past dark and I couldn't see any bottles. And I was losin' good territory. I was passin' it over. I used to clean up everything that looked like a bottle in front of me on one side of the road as I went along. Even when I got to the other end, if say I was goin' to Dannevirke; I'd look right *to*

Dannevirke. Then I'd come right back to Woodville. Twenty six miles both ways. I'd race all-comers along the way, too. And I'd win.

In fact, once I beat the army along there! There was a sergeant and another guy, they came marching along flat to the boards and they actually passed me, they caught me unawares. I thought alright matey, I won't be passin' a bottle along the way and I won't be loafin'. I set off after them.

They were only about a hundred feet ahead of me before I started to move. At one stage I was going to let them go, I was quite peaceful, and I thought they were havin' me on. But I wasn't goin' to let the army beat me, ever!

When I got level with them I said 'Where ya goin' mates?'

'Aw,' he said 'we're goin' to Dannevirke.'

I said 'Do ya expect to be there today?'

One replied 'Yeah. We expect to be there in a couple of hours.'

I said 'Well I'll tell ya what. I'll make it easier for you. Keep an eye out for me when you get further down the road - I'll have the billy boiling when you get there! That'll give you heart!'

You know what happened? They never arrived!

They got into the first car when I was up ahead and out of sight. I boiled the billy like I said I would. And I had this great big sack full of blinkin' bottles and everything imaginable, whilst they had little haversacks on their sides.

I was absolutely tireless. It was like what the prophet Isaiah said, and I must've been in that category. He said when you have the grace of God, you'll run and not grow weary, you'll walk and not grow tired, and you'll rise up with wings as angels.

Someone said once, 'But don't you ever get lonely?'

I said 'First to get lonely I have to get alone. But I never am. There's at least the two of us out there all the time, me and God.'

Just at the crucial moment when I'm fishing, and when God knows that I know it is the crucial moment, he sends someone along to *talk* to me. You get a blinkin' stingray or something huge on your hook and there's a guy tryin' to talk to you about bloody rubbish or something. So sometimes we get arguin' too. And if I'm not arguin' with God I could be arguin' with my cat. He's hungry and complaining. So there's someone there wants to talk, there's the cat, the waves are getting up so there's God and the fish slips off so I give a yell. At times there's a helluva racket goin' on. In fact at times I wish I *was* lonely.

According to the Book, the disciples were told to follow him and he'd make them fishes of men. And that's what he's prompting me to remember. Whether or not I can be a fisher of men and a fisher of fish at the same time is the big problem. Especially as I'm catchin' fish too. So there's me with one on the hook and I'm tryin' to put some sense into a guy at the same time.

I'm meeting a lot of interesting people by the way too. They just come out of the blue. You look down the beach and there's nothing there. Look the other way, nothing there. Oh thank God for that. Crikey, before you've turned around to look again, here they are right alongside you! They didn't come from the beach at all. They came from the road! Only a few yards away.

This is the way the world is. He was up there watchin' you look.

So what show have you got?

I think he knows now that I know what he's about. And he's havin' a great laugh too.

I've seen the wind go in a complete circle in sixty seconds.

I was living in the beach umbrella and it was down on a beach at Kaiaua, near Kawakawa Bay. A beautiful sunny day then almost within minutes a hell of a squall came in like a blinkin' express train, from the sea. Screamin' and blowin' like bloody hell. So I thought, well, bugger this, I'm gonna put my bit of nylon tent skirting on around the outside.

I'd just got it on. Instead of tryin' to peg it down in an emergency like that, which was a hassle to do, I took the bike panniers off and stacked them on the edges. I let the umbrella down a bit.

But this day was a real hassle day. The sea was there. The door was on the opposite side, and the wind was comin' in from the sea. Before I had all the panniers down the wind started coming from the opposite direction.

He thought He'd string me along a little bit longer. So what'd he do? He let me get all the panniers down next time. He even let me sit down. Then immediately the wind came from the sea again. Was I kept goin' 'round in circles!

Every time the wind changed I had to get out and turn the umbrella. Well, I decided. I'll sit with all the panniers all around me.

Then you discovered there was such a thing as an updraft. Something you never experienced before.

It didn't matter what you did, you had to admit there was something, havin' games with you.

And it made you shake. Because you thought, by crikey, if I'm bein' bossed around by somebody else still, well that's not what I was aimin' for. I was tryin' to get *away* from that situation.

You was up and you was down, in more ways than one. Your ego went up and down with you. Every time you did something different of course things changed radically. And you had to change with it quick.

I've seen me with nothing but an eel, one teaspoon of tea and one billy-full of water, and no more within twenty miles. I'd taken everything off the bike to make meself reasonably comfortable while I cooked the only thing I had. I had caught this eel goin' across the road, as a matter of fact, yeah, under its own steam.

So I nabbed it.

I thought gee, I hadn't a blinkin' scary of tucker, this'll do me.

So what I had to do was roast this blinkin' eel just by the fire and I had to figure out how I was goin' to do it first, even cook it, 'cause that's all I had.

Havin' figured it out I thought yeah, that'll work, now what about the tea, what's the best way to do it? And it was only about the second or third time I ever tried to make tea in a billy.

And I cried. It didn't matter what I did, I couldn't get a match lit.

I struck matchbox after matchbox, used up all me matches and I had a couple left. And she went when I got down to the last two matches.

The realisation hit me that I knew nothing about the properties of fire. It was fighting me, and telling me to do some homework. I was absolutely exhausted. Wasn't even hungry anymore. Or anything else. I was terribly upset, in every sense.

Anyway, He thought He'd have a bit more fun. He said This guy's so dumb, he needs to learn a lot faster'n I'm teachin' him. So I'll give 'im another one right now.

I just reached over to turn the blinkin' eel over and I knocked all the water I had, tea, everything else, flying, when it just got to the simmer, when I was all about to drink it. As soon as I took my hand away from the eel, I knocked it.

So my labour was all for nothing.

Next thing you're goin' to bed. Maybe you'll be beginnin' to wonder whether your big toe's gonna get wet, or your blinkin' arse or what. Well he can get you wet all at once. He can blow the whole caboodle away in one go.

It happened.

We know something about what the spirit can do. Spirit is not a thing that you manufacture yourself, it's an endowment, a gift to you. A matter of strength in a time of necessity, when you need an extra something to carry you through, that is to achieve a purpose or to carry on until the end of the task. 'Mission completed,' I used to say, at the end of the day.

I was picking up beer bottles once. I got about a dozen and I thought 'Gee, what a bloody load! You know by the time I finished I could carry about sixty on my back as well as me own gear, over thirty miles a day, and be happy about it.

I never would put one down, but would rather pick another up. If I caught myself thinking of putting one down mate, well, if there was no bottle around, I'd put a stone in my sack.

Why? Because it was a spiritual thing. I took the bull by the horns and said 'This is it matey. If you dare to think of ever weakening, you pick another up.' That cured that one. It was a very effective cure. I stopped feeling sorry for myself. If I still felt tired - another stone!

It would make a bag heavier, so you thought, just as you also thought that putting one down was going to make it lighter and found that you were wrong. But your burden is never heavy, your burden is light. That's the kind of spirit I believed in.

It was the same with food. Rather than eat when I was hungry I would often wait 'til my body was past hunger, when it wasn't dictatin' me what to do.

So when you go out in the wilds, it's not goin' to be a piece of cake. When people see me doin' things, and they think I got something, they don't see God. It was him that made me like that, but crikey, what I had to go through.

I felt it all, each time was like a father whipping his son. It was a lesson in being too careless and plain bloody dumb, in his sight, far below what he expected of his man.

This is what he would say to you, if he thought it would do any good.

Beware.

You've fooled me into believin' that what you wanted was all laid on, all mod cons and that. Well I gave you mod cons. Now I see you've had a gutsful. If you go out and do it different, take me on with the wind and the tide and the rivers and the sun, taking me on in a natural form, you'll have a new lesson. Harder than the last one.

But one thing I can't understand is this. He doesn't seem to draw the line anywhere. It seems to me it's either one extreme or the other, there's no halfways. He says if you want it I'll give it to ya, and I'll give it to ya so much that you'll wish you've never seen it. Or so little that you'll wish you rather had so much.

But I daresay up ahead I'll find he's a moderate. He could be giving me extremes to make me hate them so much that I'll actually look for that middle way and find that level. But he'll give me a few clues, short of telling me how, to find it. And I'll head in that direction.

I might even be enticed in that direction. As soon as I'm convinced I've got something, he'll convince me I haven't. Then he'll convince me that I have, when I've decided that I haven't. So on she goes, the heat's on again.

The best out of life is doing things like a kid. To us it's a piece of cake, but to a kid building a sandcastle is a new adventure and something for which they can say 'I did it all by myself mummy.' That's why a kid is so happy.

God can do all things, but that doesn't mean he will. Maybe he'd rather you did it yourself. It's more fun for him when you have the fun of achieving something. He knows the answers because he made the situation such as it is, and he can change the wind in an instant if he has the desire to, but he wants you to beat the wind. He might allow you to think that in some circumstances he could allow you to have sufficient brains to be his equal. But he wants you to do your homework and solve things without unnecessary talk, without unnecessary movement.

I used to fell trees in the bush once, but I haven't done that much living right *in* the bush. But I'm one hundred percent certain I'd survive.

There's only one thing I'm not too enthusiastic about and that's mountaineering. I'm not a great lover of heights and I'm a disliker of snow, and bare rocks don't appeal. From a distance they can be beautiful, but fighting 'ems not on, mate. I've enough to do, to work out right here.

I won't be motivated 'til I'm pushed. When I am, well then I'll move, but fast, in all ways. When the spirit moves me there's no stopping things, and certainly no half measures. And what moves me doesn't seem to be up to me.

What we think of as random, is God's idea of order. God is in opposition to the world. What we think of as order is when we're very sadly mistaken. Sometimes it's just a waste of time talkin' at all.

And yet it's interesting, that's why we do it. That's the richness of living, you don't only want to catch the fish and eat it, you want to know why, how, who put him on the hook and how often it's likely to occur and what you can do about it to make it better. It seems we can never stop thinkin'. And it doesn't matter what *people* think. The only two that matter what you're thinkin' are yourself and what you think God is.

As soon as you get up in the morning that brain machine starts workin'! As soon as I'm on the seat of me bike, I'm schemin'. I'm all go. Yet I'm enjoying every breath of fresh air as I go down the road on a beautiful morning, free as the breeze.

'Oh,' they say, 'are you going up that hill?'

'Aw, 'it's in front of me, isn't it? Eh?'

'Do you think you can get over?'

I said 'I don't even think about it. I haven't yet thought about it. I'll think about that when I'm over.'

And it's such a thrill riding hills and things I go harder at it each trip, each time comin' past. One time, rather than worry about a hill I was actually lookin' for 'em. There's nothin' more monotonous than a dead straight road.

I've only had a push-bike and within limits I could only carry so much. My mode of transport has dictated my limitations. I did have to walk with the bike, ride with the bike, park with the bike, anywhere, without any extra equipment or preparation that was already there on it, at all times.

That's why I had all telescopic stands, I still got 'em. I could park on any angle, compound angle, a gully, anywhere you like, almost upside down, I could take both wheels off and leave it there, upright. Fully loaded, standin' there with no wheels on! Nothing was left to chance, so much so that she's just as operable now as she ever was.

I paid ten dollars for this bike, every bit of twenty years ago. She's done countless thousands of miles but I've done a hell of a lot more on foot, without the bike.

I took part in a race once and I finished last. School sports, all these schools together, havin' a big sports day. And man, did I look a big fool. Miles behind the mob. But if the race'd been walkin' from Auckland to Wellington I'd'a won hands down; and it wouldn't've been long enough.

I couldn't convince anybody of that. They said 'Oh, I saw ya. You were bloody miles behind the mob. You could do better than that. I said no. I was goin' with all me heart and soul.

I'm a late starter and I'm a late finisher. You've got sprinters and you've got stayers. And you've got super-stayers. I'm that.

I'm not in a hurry along the way at all. I believe in winnin' without any hustle or bustle.

Any amount of cyclists can outrace me on the road. If they can beat that they can beat me. You can just about crawl down the road like a snail and still win. So if you know you're not a sprinter, get in a race that's a bit further, that requires a stayer. As a matter of fact, you might even die before you've finished the race. So you couldn't lose, could you! Unbeatable mate.

The greatest machines, we've forgotten, are in your own body. Even that bike can't move without my legs.

You look at the human frame, all the joints. So workable, so mechanically fantastic. A vehicle can never go up a vertical mountain.

A man can.

If he can't do it with equipment he's got, he'll make equipment that'll take 'im the full distance. Although a man grew like a flower, from something so microscopic you can hardly see it, he has to go another way about gettin' a mechanical result. He has to start with steel and he's got a helluva hassle to go through, makin' lathes and God knows what, to make those joints and all that kind of thing. And he can't even make them to compare with a biological system.

A car goes forward, so does man. But a car rolls along, on

wheels, not nearly as many bits as the action of a man running. And not up hill and down dale climbin' and jumpin'. Doesn't need a driver, the power is within it, it can run backward, forward, sideways, turn flips, even make itself fly with a few extras.

I'm the greatest machine, if you're comparing me and that, the bike's not even in the running. He hasn't done bad for a bike, but he pales into insignificance beside me! I'm the ultimate, when it comes to personal transport, I'm unbeatable!

Look, I could set off right now and head for Wellington, with every joy in my heart that I'll be there alright. I won't be rushin', but I'll get there in pretty good time in spite of myself.

I'll be livin' it up on the way too, not in the sense that most people would, callin' into every blinkin' pub and all that sort of thing. I've never called into a pub in my bloody life while I've been on the road. But I'll just be enjoying the odd campsite, and testing things out again going over old ground in some cases and relishing what I've already learnt, some of the richer things, doing them just for the sheer joy of seeing if they still work. To find if I still have the grace to do the same things would be thanks enough. Who knows what's 'round the next bend?

In two weeks' time I could be in Fiji matey, wearin' a suit!

SuperTramp

End of The Road

"Infinity is a combination of fresh air and spirit." - Bruce

The familiar dusty figure is absent from the small towns on the East Coast and its white empty beaches. People don't point and talk and wonder, and the bottles are beginning to gather again under the blackberry.

About four months before vandals pushed his carefully manicured camp and garden at Ohiwa over the cliff, Bruce was cycling along the highway just out from Opotiki when a VW Kombi stopped just ahead and the driver got out and waited for Bruce to ride up.

'Gidday,' he said.

'What's the trouble?' said Bruce, coming to a stop.

'Oh,' he said, 'I saw you up at Hicks Bay a few years ago.'

'Did you now.'

'Yes. Do you remember me?'

'You? You're just like a million more, mate.' Bruce replied. 'Crikey dick, if I remembered everybody I saw I'd need to be more than a computer! How long was I talkin' to you?'

'Oh,' the man said, 'for about half an hour or more.'

'Half an hour? You're not even in the running!' Bruce cried. 'Get way down the list! Right to the bottom, matey!'

The stranger said 'I've been looking for you all over.'

'So?'

'Well, would you get in the van? I want you to come and see my building.'

Bruce thought, he later told me, what a funny thing to say to someone you hardly know. 'Building? Me? What do I want to see your building for? Look, I'm busy. There's nothing I want to look at. I've only got half me bottles. I'm pickin' them up, that's my bread and butter. I've got to get on with it if you don't mind. And I'm in a rush right now to get home and cook tea. '

'Oh, forget the bottles. I'll give you some money. How much do you want?'

'No,' said Bruce, 'I don't do things that way. I like to earn my money, if I must.'

The man said 'Well leave your bike here and come with me.'

'Where?'

'Oh, to Opotiki.' He persisted. 'I want to show you my building.'

'But I'm not interested in bloody buildings!'

He could see the guy wasn't going to give up, so he said

'Alright. I'll come and see your building, but I'm not leaving my bike here! So somehow or other you've got to get this bike there as well, if I'm coming at all. And *that's* final.'

'We'll open up these side doors and see if we can get it in,' the man said.

In hindsight Bruce wished he'd never met John Westicott because eventually, all that followed made such an upheaval of things.

They got the bike and all the bottles in the van, although Bruce's initial reckoning was that it couldn't be done.

'I need a favour. But I'm willing to pay,' Westicott said, as they drove back toward town. 'I own premises in town. They're getting on a bit and I need an old style carpenter to do some plastering and building work using the old methods. It's been suggested that you're the very man who might be able to help me.'

'I don't work for wages.'

'But I'd pay really well.'

'Well I can't help you, sorry mate.'

Westicott was annoyed. He couldn't understand why Bruce, of no visible means, was turning down a blank cheque.

'Look,' he said, 'you're my last hope. There's no-one else around here can do the job'

'Mate,' said Bruce 'I told you I don't work for wages. Look, I'll have a look at what you want done, and I may even do some, but it will have to be on one condition and one condition only.'

'Sure, what's that?'

'That you don't pay me a cent mate. Otherwise, no deal.'

They drove to town. There was much to be done in the way of brick and stonework, some plumbing, carpentry and painting. And the work *was* just up Bruce's alley. John agreed to the condition of no wages.

So for a few weeks Bruce worked until it was finished, with John providing all the materials. Then he said 'I've got men coming to do some picking for me on my orchard on the hill, and I need a caravan refurbished for them to live in. I've got it parked at the back and I hoped you might do it up for me.'

'Okay, 'said Bruce. 'what d'ya want done? But – same deal!' And for another week or so Bruce worked on that. John was entirely pleased. At the end of that project they towed the caravan away up to his land. Bruce did some renovations too at John's home. He got on well with Mrs Westicott.

One day John said 'Bruce, I've got another caravan which will be in this same position tomorrow. I'd like that done up too.'

When it was done he said 'Thanks. It's a great job. The caravan looks beaut. Now it's yours if you want it. I'm giving it to *you*'

Bruce said 'A great big caravan is the very last thing I want mate! I'd have to pay for the paint! You have it and you pay for the bloody paint! Anyway, I haven't got a car to tow it.'

'You can leave it there.'

'That's what I propose to do.'

'Well you could live in it.'

'But I've got my own place now. Up at Ohiwa.' (The vandals hadn't been in yet)

'Well why don't you consider it your second home. Or your home when you come into town. I'll leave it here anyway, and if not the owner, you could be the caretaker of it.'

'There's only one Caretaker,' said Bruce, 'and I could never do his job. And I know He'd be very annoyed if he knew that I was after it! But matey, I'm prepared to watch over it if I'm around.'

And so it was. Bruce stayed one night in it, then another, on occasions when it was too late in the day to cycle the thirty-minute ride back home. And then, by some fluke of timing, the vandal attack, which saw Bruce move into town while he thought of what to do next.

As soon as he had more or less moved in to the caravan, John showed up. He took Bruce into every shop in Opotiki. To each shop-owner he said 'This is Bruce. Anything he wants, give it to him. On my account!' Because Bruce had totalled up a couple of thousand, if not more, in unpaid wages.

So Bruce and his cat were in clover for a while. They had bacon and eggs every morning for breakfast and jelly-meat was on tap. Bruce acquired tools, and clothing.

He began to sense he'd won a significant moral victory, although he wasn't sure over whom. He reasoned that the vandals had been locals, maybe high officials of the town and still out to get him, and still even more desirous of moving him on - but now they knew once again where he was hiding.

'They can't do a bloody thing about it, mate!' he said to me. 'I'm here legitimately. I don't own it, yet I've full rights to occupy. So the wheel has come full circle. You couldn't get a more perfect situation. I've moved back to living in a town but it's not costing me a cracker! Not a cent. And I'm not in the suburbs or anything. I'm dead bang near the middle of the main street. Right in the bloody hornets' nest!'

'There's a certain day coming, matey. If I ever see any glory in my life I'll see some on that particular day. And I don't think it's too far off just now either. I'm goin' to see it right here. When I put this whole supermarket car park into spuds.'

Bruce started putting on weight. Not needing to rush around on the bike meant he was getting little or no exercise. Plus the bacon and steak he was eating every day, fried in fat.

'I only do things out of necessity,' he said. 'In this way of livin' I've no need to exercise. Me tucker's right here. And in quantity. If I need to fish I just fish under the bed for a tin of something!' As usual, his logic was flawless.

I returned to Auckland and checked out some of what he had told me over the years. I found his sister Pat and her husband Fred, two delightful elderly folk who had spent a lifetime of worrying about their eccentric relative. Yes, he had camped at their place in

Point Chev, in the backyard, when he came to town, but when he was coming or when he was leaving was always unknown in advance.

Bruce had noted to me once, as if in warning, 'I never tell people when I'm coming, or when I'm going, for that matter. I just disappear, fade away. I know quite often that people are relieved when I do, too. They get a bit bored with me sometimes. You can be overbearing without knowing it. Not everyone is as enthusiastic as you are about everything'.

'I never write to anyone, not even to my own family; what's left. I like them to come and see me or I visit them, if I'm around.

But people aren't dead as far as I'm concerned. It's just a curtain between them and me. I know they're still around but I know I can never contact them in the sense that we can contact as human beings. But they can contact us. I have very close contact with my mother. Although I don't know for sure that she's dead, I do know that she's with me every day and she tells me so. So whether she's alive or dead is no different. There's really no such thing. This person is not necessarily a mother in the sense we understand a mother. This person is as Christ said when he was tackled about something about his mother. My mother? The same as my sister or my brother, carrying out the will of higher forces. So it's in that form. I see my mother pretty well every day. She's not here and yet she's here. Yet again there's no reason why she should be because I was brought up as an orphan.'

Apart from when Pat and Fred went down country in a camper

and stayed with Bruce on the coast a couple of times, mostly they didn't know where he was. His habit of sometimes getting into trouble kept them in a state of continual concern.

I took the ferry to Waiheke and found that the ladies he mentioned had long passed. And I gathered newspaper reports of Bruce's sightings, and the odd story or two from locals around the place who remembered Bruce, but I found that because of the passage of time, most of whom Bruce referred me to had moved away. passed away or were by now of unknown whereabouts.

Armed with at least some information, even about deaths that I thought Bruce might want to know about, I drove down to update him.

In Opotiki the caravan was deserted, just an empty shell. Clearly, nobody had occupied it for some time.

I rang Westicott. Apparently there'd been some trouble and Bruce was asked to leave. Relations between them both were rather strained at the moment, he said.

Well where was Bruce? He hadn't a clue. But he said he heard that Bruce now has *a Toyota Hi-Ace van.*

A van is easier to find than a single camouflaged person hiding in the undergrowth somewhere on the whole East Coast. It didn't take me long. I went down each beach and byway south of the town. I knew he wouldn't have moved far in that short a time. I knew too that he would be on or near a beach. Then again, perhaps he *was* in Fiji!

As I passed Torere Beach, some ten miles from Opotiki, I glanced seaward. I saw a cream Hi-Ace van poking above the low scrub. It was the only vehicle in the deserted area and it had all manner of pipes and containers on the roof rack - like a more complex version of panniers on a bike. It had to be him. I drove in and parked right beside it. There was nobody around. Then a curtain moved and parted, and I saw the familiar bearded face.

He was very excited to see me because he had been a bit down. What a lot he had to tell me. There'd been a spot of bother with John. Firstly, yahoos trying to get into the caravan in town had been giving Bruce sleepless nights. The council had wanted Bruce out of there but no-one was prepared to ask him to leave. It was finally up to Westicott to deliver the marching orders. Talk about betrayal.

And he'd been in touch with sister Pat.

I'd a lot to tell him too. I said 'I thought you might like to know that Mrs Wells on Waiheke passed away five years ago.'

He said 'Well actually I wouldn't like to know that matey. But I did suspect it would be the case.'

Then I heard that Pat and John and one or two others from the town had talked him into cashing in his superannuation arrears. To begin with he had put up resistance. 'All these years of *not* havin' it is the tax I been payin' for the right to be left alone,' he'd always said. Now what was he to tell people if he picked up on it?

But Pat and John kept on. In the end he went along with them, if just to shut them up. Even though he had a bundle owing that he hadn't picked up for years, he was only given the standard maximum arrears pay-out, a fraction of what he was due. It amounted to a couple of thousand.

So he bought the van. But he couldn't drive. It had been thirty-five years since he'd sat behind a wheel. However, being Bruce, he had a plan. He would hitchhike in reverse! He would wait in the van beside the road for a hitch-hiker to happen by. He would flag down the hitchhiker, who would drive to where he or she wanted to go, Eketahuna or whatever, and then Bruce's wait beside the road for the *next* hitchhiker to come along. That way he figured he'd get around the country and not be breaking the law..

And at the moment, he said, he's still gettin' the van ready for this trip.

He was thinking, too, of building a little shed out of concrete blocks for himself, on a mate's bit of land on the outskirts of the town. He'd planned for this in detail. To avoid getting a building permit, which was unnecessary and expensive, he was going to buy the blocks and other materials, take them up one at a time in a covered bag and stack them out of sight 'til he was ready. Wouldn't he get reported? Building inspectors, he reasoned, only take notice of buildings under construction, not those already up. So when he'd gotten everything all ready, one night it would mushroom into being. Completely finished by morning. An overnight cabin.

The van was a typical Bruce masterpiece of planning. The bed was all along one side, and on the other was the woodstove, sink, and cupboards. They were arranged so that he could cook and eat breakfast without getting out of bed. The wood stove was built by him too, basically a short fat L-shaped pipe. He'd also planned and started to build a steam driven dynamo as part of the wetback system. He was working to a drawing of the turbines the ocean liners use, coupled to their huge diesels. Only this one was a tiny miniature.

Everything was on go ahead. His excitement reminded me of the time he was building his cube caravan. There were even some bottles stacked against the van, and I saw the old bike leaning against the headlight. He'd gone back to getting some bottles, on the bike, leaving the van as base. Not in any big way, more as exercise than anything else.

Shortly before Christmas he went into town to get provisions. He could drive, though only slowly, and his eyesight and his hearing, he knew, were not good enough for him to travel any sort of long distance. Also, he had no license or warrant, so he wasn't prepared to go any further afield.

Once a week he was doing this ten mile trip. He would shop for himself and the cat, call in to chat with some of his acquaintances in the shops, and crawl back to Torere. The law had by now long tolerated him anyway. In fact two policemen had told me where his camp was. I never told Bruce that.

By now I was back in Auckland.

On one of these trips to town he felt a little odd. Often he would not have minded the odd chest pain, putting it down to some message to ease up, or poisoned fungi. He did not consider anything to be really serious. But walking down Opotiki's main street he collapsed.

He was wide awake as they took him to the hospital for tests.

Imagine the horror it was to wake up lying in a hospital bed. Captivity. His cat wasn't getting fed. He had things to get on with.

After a day of observation the hospital let him go. They told him to take it easy. He went back to the beach.

But the next day he took a turn for the worse. This is really telling me something, he reasoned. Tellin' me to go back to that hospital for more blinkin' tests.

According to the reception records of the 19th of December, he readmitted himself to the Opotiki Hospital. That night Bruce died.

He would've decided to, like the Maori chief he had found in the bush. He knew he could never go back to the road now in the same old way. It was behind him. Even though the bike was hanging on a bracket on the back of the van in readiness, his body had been slowly packing up for a while.

His eyes and hearing were getting unreliable, his teeth and heart gave him unexplained pains and he was enormously unfit.

He started to realize that his body was finally beginning to fail him and he was being forced into giving himself in, tricked even, thinking 'okay God, I get the bloody message, you want my body? Well you take it!'

This was his way of putting a perspective on it. And in this final defiance was the symmetry of humility, of loving God, of knowing that he had been cared for all those years and was still being watched over, and that there was everything to gain still and never anything to lose.

He'd had in his mind an idea of what he wanted to do. It started off as a huge and to him a mighty dream, and somehow he'd taken courage and done it. For sure he'd lived his dream. No one anywhere could say he hadn't. All those years ago, when he could see no way possible to do so, he'd moved forward, taken the first step, taken the second one, taken the third, every one had been one less. And with the help of a supreme Teacher, only the best, he'd made it more than a dream, he'd made it a reality.

So what more was there to be done? The real dream was to fulfil the dream, to see if it could be done, because any challenge overcome was essentially the nature of challenge itself. No man had done more, and there was no more that this man had to do. All that was left to have filled his heart was the very private feeling of pure thanks, for the richness of what his living had been, and the looking ahead of the gift of himself to his Lord.

> **Quiet funeral**
> Tauranga Staff
>
> When the body of 71-year-old Bruce Davenport Collins is lowered into his grave in the Opotiki cemetery this afternoon the only witness will be a police officer.
>
> Mr Collins was a drifter who had lived in a small van in the Opotiki district for the past two years.
>
> Sometimes he camped on beaches and sometimes in camping grounds.
>
> When he fell ill recently he was admitted to Opotiki Hospital, but he discharged himself.
>
> Last Tuesday he took a turn for the worse and returned to the hospital, where he died that night.
>
> The Opotiki police have been unable to discover any relatives, although Mr Collins is supposed to have a sister, a Mrs Robinson, in Auckland.
>
> Nor have they been able to establish much about his past, except that he probably came to Opotiki from Auckland.
>
> Though he was an itinerant with a simple way of life, Mr Collins was not a pauper.
>
> A bank account checked by the police had a balance of $8800.
>
> With no known relatives, Mr Collins' estate will go to the Public Trustee, and with no known friends there will be no mourners at his funeral today.

NZ Herald 22/12/1989

I saw this and rang Pat. She'd seen it too, contacted the authorities, and was already packing to go down.

The following day this article appeared in the same newspaper:

> **Sister found**
> Tauranga Staff
>
> The funeral of 71-year-old Bruce Davenport Collins in Opotiki yesterday was not the lonely affair it might have been.
>
> With no known relatives and no close friends, it looked as if a police officer might be the only witness.
>
> But when Mr Collins' sister, Mrs Patricia Robinson of Auckland, read a report of Mr Collins' lonely death in yesterday's issue of the *New Zealand Herald*, she contacted the Opotiki police.
>
> The story was the first she knew of the death of her brother, a drifter who lived in a small van in the Opotiki district for the past two years.
>
> The funeral was postponed so Mrs Robinson and her son could attend.
>
> In the meantime, the police had ascertained that Mr Collins had undertaken military service abroad, and members of the Opotiki Returned Services Association also attended the funeral yesterday afternoon.

NZ Herald 23/12/1989

About 50 people turned up and the local RSA gave him an honourable military send-off. Mention was made that he was not just a soldier but one of life's true fighters. It was a fitting tribute.

SuperTramp

Acknowledgements

There are many who have helped bring this book to its final form. Thank you Pat and Fred Robinson, for your filling in of so many gaps, your empathy with the task in hand and your permission to reveal personal family information.

Thank you Kim and Odette for photos and little snippets. And Jack Leigh too, of the Auckland Star, for permission to reprint your photos.

Thanks too to Mary Crockett for her considerable editing help and wise suggestions.

And a huge thanks to dear friend Mike Colonna who took Bruce's story to his heart and devoted much free time in assisting me reposition text.

Finally, of course, Bruce.

www.ingramcontent.com/pod-product-compliance
Lightning Source LLC
Chambersburg PA
CBHW051749040426
42446CB00007B/284